THE
DRUMS AND PERCUSSION
COOKBOOK
Creative Recipes
for Players and Teachers

Published by
Meredith Music Publications
a division of G.W. Music, Inc.
4899 Lerch Creek Ct., Galesville, MD 20765
http://www.meredithmusic.com

Copyright © 2008 MEREDITH MUSIC PUBLICATIONS
International Copyright Secured • All Rights Reserved
First Edition
October 2008

International Standard Book Number: 978-1-57463-101-2
Printed and bound in U.S.A.

Contents

Foreword

Having a "cookbook" for drummers and percussionists makes a lot of sense. Many drummers tell a stereotypical story of starting out by banging on their mother's pots and pans, and early trap kits were often described as consisting of everything but the kitchen sink. During my symphonic years, a conductor used to routinely refer to the percussion section (which, of course, included kettle drums) as the kitchen. Max Roach wrote a drum solo called "The Pies of Quincy" in honor of his Zildjian cymbals, which, as part of their manufacturing process are baked in ovens. African djembes are said to have originated when someone stretched a goatskin head over the hourglass-shaped mortar that women used to beat grain into flour, and some of the traditional rhythms are attributed to patterns the women created while beating the grain with pestles. And the highest praise you can give drumset players is to tell them that they are "cookin'."

It seems very appropriate, then, to present a set of "recipes" from some of the finest players and teachers in the drum and percussion world. Each author was asked to contribute an article on a subject he or she was passionate about, and the results have combined into a smorgasbord of advice covering a wide range of topics, including physical and mental practicing, technical and stylistic development, auditions, contests, teaching, interpretation, and performing, and covering such genres as rock, jazz, classical percussion, marching percussion, and hand drumming. Some of the recipes are specific to an instrument; others can be applied to just about any musician's life.

My thanks to Gar Whaley for inviting me to coordinate this project. Of all the drum books I've edited over the past 25 years, this one is the most unique. Thanks especially to the authors who contributed their recipes; it has been an honor and inspiration to work with all of you, and I'm sure that your contributions herein will feed the drum and percussion community for many decades to come.

Rick Mattingly

Acknowledgments

To each of the *chefs* who contributed to this publication, I offer my sincere thanks. Each individual responded to our initial invitation with a resounding yes. They were each enthusiastic about being involved in what they felt would be a unique and worthwhile contribution to percussion playing and to music education. Their generosity has been exceptional, their expertise unquestionable and their love of percussion playing and music education inspiring. The writings within, presented by them, are based on years of study and experience from a variety of educational and professional levels.

Profound thanks and admiration are extended to Rick Mattingly, editor and coordinator of this volume. Rick could, and should, write a book on organization and management; his skills are incredible! He is a creative and talented individual to whom I owe a great deal of thanks for his tireless work on this project. Rick went about the task of selecting authors, organizing and collecting materials, motivating writers and editing text with energy and enthusiasm. In addition to being an outstanding musician, Rick is also an educator and author of the highest order which is apparent in the composition of this volume. Thanks to Rick Mattingly, the world now has a collection of interesting and insightful articles contained in one volume written by many of today's most outstanding percussion players and pedagogues. To Shawn Girsberger my unending gratitude for her work with Meredith Music Publications and for the artistic layout and cover design of this volume. To the Percussive Arts Society, its leaders and members, my unyielding thanks for the incredible difference this exceptional organization has played in leading percussion education world wide.

And finally, to the thousands of drum and percussion students and their teachers who have inspired each of us, our never-ending thanks for your dedication, beautiful music making and the belief that music does make a difference.

Garwood Whaley
President and Founder
Meredith Music Publications

∾ ∾ ∾

About the Authors

Kenny Aronoff has toured and/or recorded with John Mellencamp, Smashing Pumpkins, Bob Seger, Melissa Etheridge, Jon Bon Jovi, Elton John, Bob Dylan, Rod Stewart, Alanis Morissette, The Rolling Stones, Lynyrd Skynyrd, Willie Nelson, Waylon Jennings, Avril Lavigne, John Fogerty, Joe Cocker, Mick Jagger, Alice Cooper, Meat Loaf, Bonnie Raitt, Santana, and many others. Kenny was named #1 Pop/Rock Drummer and #1 Studio Drummer for five consecutive years by the readers of *Modern Drummer* magazine.

Anders Åstrand is active as a mallet artist, clinician, and composer. He regularly performs recitals and gives clinics throughout the U.S. and Europe, both as a mallet soloist and with his percussion ensemble, Global Percussion Network. In his compositions, Åstrand focuses on improvisation as an essential feature for soloists as well as the ensemble. Since 2002, Åstrand has served on the Board of Directors for the Percussive Arts Society.

John H. Beck is Professor of Percussion at the Eastman School of Music and retired Timpanist of the Rochester Philharmonic Orchestra. He is active throughout the United States, Europe, and South America as a performer, composer, clinician, and conductor. He has published numerous articles in professional journals and written many solos and instructional books for percussion. He is a past president of the Percussive Arts Society and a member of the PAS Hall of Fame.

Alessandra Belloni is the artistic director, founder, and lead performer of I Giullari di Piazza, an Italian music, theatre, and dance ensemble who are artists-in-residence at the Cathedral of St. John the Divine in New York City. She is author of the book/DVD package *Rhythm is the Cure*, published by Mel Bay. Belloni was born in Rome, Italy, and is committed to preserving the strong and rich traditions of her native culture.

Ivana Bilic is principal timpanist of the Symphony Orchestra of the Croatian Radio and on faculty at the Zagreb Music Academy. She received a Porin Award (the prestigious Croatian Discographic Award) for best classical performance in 2001 for her solo CD *Follow Me* and in 2004 for her solo performance of the marimba concerto by I. Kuljeric on the CD *Igor Kuljeric – Contemporary Croatian Composers*. Ivana is the author of several marimba solos and a duo published by Malletworks.

Bob Breithaupt is Professor of Music and Department Chair of Music Business & Industry Studies at Capital University. He is the co-director of the Summer Drumset Workshops, author of the textbook *The Complete Percussionist* and the DVD *Snare Drum Basics*, and a past president of the Percussive Arts Society. He has performed with such artists as Benny Carter, Terry Gibbs, John Pizzarelli, and Monty Alexander, and has served as the drummer of the Columbus Jazz Orchestra since 1980.

Bill Bruford played with progressive rock groups Yes, King Crimson, Genesis, and UK. His groups Bruford and Earthworks led the way with advanced harmony in electric rock in the 1970s and '80s; samples, electronics, and odd-meters in electric jazz in the '90s; and stylistic innovation with strong compositional identity in his current 21st-century acoustic jazz. His life's work is well documented on CD and DVD at Summerfold and Winterfold Records and at www.billbruford.com.

Michael Burritt is Professor of Percussion at the Eastman School of Music, and a percussion soloist and pedagogue, specializing in marimba. He has written two concertos as well as solo and chamber works for marimba, percussion, and percussion ensemble, and has recorded three solo compact discs. He has served on the Percussive Arts Society Board of Directors and as chair of the PAS Keyboard Committee, and has been a featured artist at numerous PASICs.

Bill Cahn has been a member of Nexus since 1971 and an Artist In Residence at the Showa Music Academy in Japan since 1998. He was Principal Percussionist in the Rochester Philharmonic Orchestra from 1968 to 1995, and a Visiting Assistant Professor of Percussion at the Eastman School of Music in 2006.

Jeff Calissi is an assistant professor of music at Eastern Connecticut State University. He received a Bachelor of Music in Music Education degree from Radford University, and Master of Music and Doctor of Musical Arts in Performance degrees from the University of North Carolina at Greensboro. Jeff has presented at the Percussive Arts Society's international convention, PASIC, is an associate keyboard editor for *Percussive Notes* journal, and serves on the PAS Scholarly Research Committee.

James Campbell is Professor of Music and Director of Percussion Studies at the University of Kentucky. A past president of the Percussive Arts Society, James maintains an active career as a performer, composer, and pedagogue.

Anthony J. Cirone was percussionist with the San Francisco Symphony and as Assistant Professor of Music at San José State University from 1965–2001. Cirone has also been on the faculty of San Francisco State University and Stanford University, and was Professor of Music and Chairman of the Percussion Department in the Jacobs School of Music at Indiana University from 2001–07. He has approximately 100 published titles, including textbooks, three symphonies for percussion, four sonatas, a string quartet, and nine works for orchestra and band.

F. Michael Combs is Professor Emeritus at the University of Tennessee where he taught percussion for four decades. He has served the Percussive Arts Society in a number of capacities and positions including hosting two PASIC conventions and editing *The Percussionist* and *Percussive Notes* magazines. He plays timpani in the Knoxville Symphony Orchestra and serves the profession in a variety of ways including doing reviews of new music for *Percussive Notes*.

Christopher Deane is Associate Professor of Percussion at the University of North Texas. He is a member of the Pulsus Percussion Group and is an active freelance percussionist in the Dallas-Ft. Worth Area. Deane has written a number of compositions for percussion that are considered standard recital repertoire. He has won both first and second prize in the PAS Composition Contest and has served on the Board of Directors of the Percussive Arts Society.

Dennis DeLucia has appeared as an expert analyst/commentator on the telecast of the DCI Championships on ESPN2 and the Regal Cinema chain since 1994. He has taught and written for such corps and bands as the Muchachos (Hawthorne, NJ), the Bridgemen (Bayonne, NJ), the Star of Indiana (Bloomington, IN), the Sunrisers (Long Island, NY), and the Caballeros (Hawthorne, NJ). His honors include the World Drum Corps Hall of Fame, Drum Corps International Hall of Fame, and the WGI Percussion Hall of Fame.

Robin Engelman is a member of Nexus and the Percussive Arts Society Hall of Fame.

Peter Erskine has played with (among others) Stan Kenton, Weather Report, Steely Dan, Steps Ahead, Joni Mitchell, Diana Krall, Kenny Wheeler, Patrick Williams, Pat Metheny,

John Abercrombie, Bill Frisell, John Scofield, and Jan Garbarek, and has appeared with the London, Los Angeles, Scottish Chamber, BBC Symphony and Berlin Philharmonic orchestras. He authored *The Erskine Method* book + DVD, *Drumming Essentials*, Volumes 1, 2 and 3, and *Time Awareness for All Musicians* (Alfred Publishing) and *Drum Concepts and Techniques* (Hal Leonard).

Neal Flum is the Associate Director of Athletic Bands at the University of Alabama in Tuscaloosa. He has served as president and secretary of the Percussive Arts Society Alabama Chapter and as interim chair of the PAS Marching Percussion Committee. Neal is also a staff member of Thom Hannum's Mobile Percussion Seminar.

Mark Ford is the coordinator of percussion activities at The University of North Texas in Denton, Texas and a past president of the Percussive Arts Society. He regularly presents marimba clinics and concerts in the U.S. and abroad.

Guy G. Gauthreaux II was principal timpanist with the United State Navy Band from 1987–2007, and he continues to teach and present clinics throughout the United States, and is an active freelance and recording percussionist in the Baton Rouge and New Orleans areas. His published compositions include solo works for snare drum, marimba, and timpani and have placed three times in the Percussive Arts Society Composition Contest. He founded Pioneer Percussion, a publishing company that specializes in advanced percussion literature.

Danny Gottlieb has recorded and/or performed with the Pat Metheny Group, Gary Burton, Chick Corea, Bobby McFerrin, Gil Evans, Sting, John McLaughlin, David Byrne, Herbie Hancock, Wayne Shorter, the Manhattan Transfer, and many more. Danny frequently performs and records with the NDR Radio Band of Hamburg, Germany, and with actor Gary Sinise's Lt. Dan Band. Danny is an Assistant Professor of Jazz Studies at the University of North Florida and a guest adjunct drumset instructor at Rollins College.

Gordon Gottlieb has had a varied career that has included performing with the New York Philharmonic, Stevie Wonder, and Miles Davis, recording with Michael Jackson, Steely Dan (*Two Against Nature*, *Everything Must Go*, solo albums with Donald Fagen and Walter Becker) and Sting, playing with an escola de samba in the carnival parade in Rio de Janeiro, recording Stravinsky's "Les Noces," "Histoire du Soldat" and "Renard" with Robert Craft, and teaching at Juilliard and Yale.

Neil Grover has performed with the Boston Symphony Orchestra and the Boston Pops as well as with rock band Aerosmith and on the soundtrack of *Indiana Jones & The Temple of Doom*. He is a popular clinician and the author of *Four Mallet Primer* and co-author (with Garwood Whaley) of *Triangle, Tambourine and Cymbal Technique*, both published by Meredith Music. He is Founder and President of Grover Pro Percussion and served on the Board of Directors of the Percussive Arts Society.

Julie Hill is Director of Percussion Studies at the University of Tennessee at Martin. She is a frequent guest lecturer and performer on the topic of Brazilian percussion. Hill serves on the international advisory board for Escola Dida, a project in Salvador da Bahia, Brazil, dedicated to social transformation for women and at-risk children through music.

Rich Holly is Professor of Percussion and Associate Dean of the College of Visual and Performing Arts at Northern Illinois University. As a performer he has appeared as a guest artist at colleges, universities, and percussion festivals throughout the world, and served as President of the Percussive Arts Society from 2005–06.

Steve Houghton is a jazz drummer, percussionist, clinician, author, and educator who has performed and recorded with Woody Herman, John Williams, Toshiko Akiyoshi, Bob Florence, Bill Holman, Freddie Hubbard, Gary Burton, Lyle Mays, Pat LaBarbara, Joe Henderson, Dianne Reeves and Karrin Allyson, among others. He is professor of jazz and percussion at Indiana University and a member of the executive committee of the Percussive Arts Society. He has recorded several solo albums and written more than 20 composite educational tools.

Arthur Hull is an internationally renowned percussionist. He is regarded by many as the person who conceived and developed the idea of the facilitated community drum circle. He has authored two books on drum circle facilitation and has traveled the world training over 3,500 drum circle facilitators. For more information, visit www.drumcircle.com.

Kalani is a professional percussionist, Orff-Schulwerk practitioner, award-winning author, and Drum Circle Music™ trainer. For more information visit kalanimusic.com and drumcirclemusic.com.

Glenn Kotche is the drummer/percussionist in the Grammy-Award-winning band Wilco. He records extensively, appearing on over 70 albums to date, and tours throughout the world. In 2006, *Mobile*, Kotche's third solo percussion record, was released on Nonesuch Records. He has been a featured performer at the Modern Drummer Festival and PASIC, and is a contributor to *Modern Drummer* and *Percussive Notes* magazines. Kotche holds a degree in Percussion Performance from the University of Kentucky.

Lalo is a vibraphonist and composer who began studying with Mike Mainieri while she was in high school and graduated from Berklee College of Music *summa cum laude*. Lalo has toured throughout the U.S. and Europe as a performer, bandleader, and clinician; recorded with jazz pianist Kenny Werner; performed with Cyro Baptista's ten-piece percussion ensemble; and regularly plays in several established New York City bands. Lalo has three albums available: *Urban Myth*, *Half Moon*, and *Lalo*.

Rick Mattingly is Publications Editor for the Percussive Arts Society. His articles have appeared in *Percussive Notes*, *Modern Drummer*, *Modern Percussionist*, *Drum!*, *Down Beat*, *Jazziz*, *Musician*, and *Pointe* magazines, and *The New Grove Dictionary of Jazz*. He is author of the books *All About Drums*, *The Drummer's Time*, and *Creative Timekeeping*, and co-author (with Rod Morgenstein) of *The Drumset Musician* and (with Blake Neely) *FastTrack Drums* vols. 1 and 2, all published by Hal Leonard Corporation.

William Moersch is Professor and Chair of Percussion Studies at the University of Illinois at Urbana-Champaign. Since 1980, he has been a leading force in the commission and performance of new repertoire for marimba by many of the most prominent composers of our time. More recently, he has also discovered a deep love for orchestral timpani and is currently Principal Timpanist/Percussionist of Sinfonia da Camera.

Jeff Moore is a Professor of Music and the Director of Percussion Studies at the University of Central Florida in Orlando. He is an Associate Editor or *Percussive Notes*, author of the book *Drumstick Control*, and a contributing author to Gary Cook's *Teaching Percussion*. He is an international performer and clinician and has appeared throughout the United States, Europe, Japan, Thailand, and Indonesia.

Rod Morgenstein is an original member of the six-time Grammy-nominated fusion band Dixie Dregs, heavy metal band Winger, prog power duo Rudess Morgenstein Project, jam band Jazz Is Dead, and muso power-pop group Jelly Jam. He is also an associate professor of percussion at Berklee College of Music.

Valerie Dee Naranjo was the first woman permitted to perform the African marimba gyil, and only Westerner to receive a first prize at Ghana's prestigious Kobine Festival. She performs, teaches, and gives clinics on six continents, including in New York City with the *Saturday Night Live* band, Broadway's *The Lion King*, Philip Glass, the Paul Winter Consort, Zakir Hussain, and others. She has six CDs and a series of 13 marimba transcriptions titled *West African Music for the Marimba Soloist* to her credit.

Mark Nauseef has performed and/or recorded with such artists as Jack Bruce, Trilok Gurtu, Steve Swallow, L. Shankar, Hamza El Din, Tony Oxley, Rabih Abou-Khalil and Lou Harrison. Nauseef studied Javanese Gamelan with K.R.T. Wasitodiningrat, Balinese Gamelan with I. Nyoman Wenten, North Indian Pakhawaj drumming and theory with Pandit Taranath Rao and Pandit Amiya Dasgupta, Ghanaian drumming and dance with Kobla and Alfred Ladzekpo, Dzidzorgbe Lawluvi, and C.K. Ganyo, and hand drumming with John Bergamo and Glen Velez.

Terry O'Mahoney is Associate Professor of Music at St. Francis Xavier University in Antigonish (Nova Scotia), Canada and is active as a performer, adjudicator, and clinician throughout the U.S. and Canada. He has performed with numerous jazz artists including Phil Woods, Curtis Fuller, Jimmy Heath, Lew Soloff, and others in addition to Symphony Nova Scotia. He is author of *Motivic Drumset Soloing - A Guide to Creative Phrasing and Improvisation*, published by Hal Leonard.

Jim Payne has authored *The Great Drummers of R&B, Funk & Soul +100 Famous Funk Beats* (formerly *Give the Drummers Some*), *Funk Drumming*, and *Tito Puente – King of Latin Music*. He has produced records for Medeski, Martin & Wood, the J.B. Horns, Fred Wesley, and Mike Clark, and has played with the J.B. Horns, Maceo Parker, Dave Liebman, and Slickaphonics. He teaches in New York City and performs and records with his group, the Jim Payne Band.

Al Payson is a retired percussionist with the Chicago Symphony Orchestra. He was elected to the PAS Hall of Fame and is a faculty member of DePaul University, where his duties include teaching a graduate level course in percussion pedagogy.

Jeff Queen is a four-time world champion snare drummer and original cast member of the Broadway show *Blast!* Queen holds his BM in Music Composition from Butler University and is the author of *The Next Level: Rudimental Snare Drum Techniques* and *Playing With Sticks*. Jeff is a highly sought-after clinician, arranger, composer, and judge who has traveled around the globe sharing his passion for music and percussion.

John Riley is a jazz drummer and Grammy-award winning recording artist with such artists as John Scofield, Mike Stern, Woody Herman, Dizzy Gillespie, Stan Getz and Miles Davis. He performs regularly with the Vanguard Jazz Orchestra, Bob Mintzer, Jon Faddis, and Joe Lovano. Riley is on the faculty of Manhattan School of Music and SUNY-Purchase and has written three critically acclaimed books about jazz drumming: *The Art of Bop Drumming*, *Beyond Bop Drumming*, and *The Jazz Drummer's Workshop*.

Lisa Rogers is Associate Professor of Percussion Studies at Texas Tech University where she teaches applied studies and directs ensembles such as the Texas Tech Steel Drum Ensemble—*Apocalypso Now*. She attended Texas State University, Texas Tech University, and University of Oklahoma for her undergraduate and graduate studies. Rogers' interest in keyboard percussion led to the release of her solo vibraphone CD recording, *Paint Me A Sky*, in January 2000.

Michael Rosen is Professor of Percussion at Oberlin Conservatory of Music and Director of the Oberlin Percussion Institute. He was Principal Percussionist with the Milwaukee Symphony from 1966–72 and has performed with the Grand Teton Music Festival, the Cleveland Orchestra, the Metropolitan Opera Orchestra, and the Concertgebouw Orchestra. He is an Associate Editor of *Percussive Notes* and has recorded for Opus One, Bayerische Rundfunk, Albany, Lumina, and CRI labels.

Ed Saindon has been teaching at Berklee College of Music since 1976 and is active as a clinician. On his latest CD, *Depth of Emotion*, Ed is featured on vibes, marimba, and piano along with saxophonist Dave Liebman. Ed is the jazz mallet-keyboard editor for *Percussive Notes* magazine.

Dave Samuels is recognized for his fresh new sound and creative approach to vibraphone and marimba. Dave has gained world wide recognition by performing and recording with such artists as Gerry Mulligan, Oscar Peterson, Chet Baker, Stan Getz, Carla Bley, The Yellowjackets, Pat Metheny, Bruce Hornsby, Frank Zappa, Spyro Gyra, and Double Image. He received a Grammy Award for "Best Latin Jazz Recording" in 2003 for *The Gathering* with his group, the Caribbean Jazz Project.

Casey Scheuerell is an Associate Professor of Percussion at Berklee College of Music where he teaches the course "Advanced Chart Reading." He is the author of *Stickings and Orchestrations for Drum Set*, available through Berklee Press. Casey has recorded and performed with many artists including Chaka Khan, Jean Luc Ponty, Robben Ford, and the Greg Hopkins Big Band.

James A. Sewrey is a charter member of the American School Band Directors Association and the author/consultant of drum studies and solos for various publications. He was a founding member of the Percussive Arts Society and author of its name. He has served as a percussionist with a variety of concert/symphonic bands and orchestras, and is a percussion educator, clinician, conductor, studio teacher, and music industry consultant.

Ed Shaughnessy has performed with every major symphony in the United States, countless big bands, and recorded with a variety of ensembles. After 29 years with the NBC *Tonight Show* orchestra, he still performs with the Doc Severinsen Orchestra and with his own 17-piece band, Energy Force. Shaughnessy has performed on over 500 albums and he won the Best Big Band Drummer category in *Modern Drummer* magazine's Readers Poll seven times.

Kristen Shiner McGuire is Coordinator of Percussion Studies at Nazareth College of Rochester. She has received the Excellence in Undergraduate Teaching Award and the Outstanding PAS Chapter President Award. Kristen is a performer on all percussion instruments and a jazz singer. She is a member of the Maelstrom Percussion Ensemble, the Elle Jazz Trio, the Rochester Philharmonic Orchestra, and the Stone Ojo Band, among others. She is also a published author and composer.

Dick Sisto performs at the famous Seelbach Hotel in Louisville, where regional and national artists often join him. He has also played gigs and given clinics with Dave Samuels, Bobby Broom, Melvin Rhyne, and Larry Koonse, and he has performed at PASIC. Sisto is the author of *The Jazz Vibraphone Book*, published by Meredith Music, and he has released several CDs, including *Soul Searching*, which includes music written for the Thomas Merton documentary bearing the same title.

Ed Soph is Professor of Music at the University of North Texas. He has toured and recorded with the big bands of Stan Kenton, Bill Watrous, Woody Herman, and Clark Terry. Small group recordings include Joe Henderson, Clark Terry, Bobby Shew, Randy Brecker, David Liebman, Carl Fontana, Marvin Stamm, Joe Locascio, and Stefan Karlsson. Ed is the author of *The Big Band Primer*, *Essential Techniques for Drum Set*, and *Musical Time* (book and DVD).

Gary Stith is conductor of the Symphonic Winds and Coordinator of Music Education at the Greatbatch School of Music at Houghton College. He holds degrees from The Ohio State University and the Eastman School of Music. He studied with John Beck, Cloyd Duff, James L. Moore, John Rowland, Goerge Ward, and William Youhass and is a frequent percussion clinician and adjudicator.

John Tafoya is Professor of Music (percussion) at Indiana University's Jacob School of Music. He served as principal timpanist of the National Symphony Orchestra from 1999–2007 and has held previous principal timpani positions with the American Wind Symphony, the National Repertory Orchestra, the Owensboro Symphony (KY), the Evansville Philharmonic Orchestra (IN) and the Florida Philharmonic Orchestra. He has also performed with the Indianapolis Symphony Orchestra and the Saint Louis Symphony Orchestra.

Garwood Whaley is President and Founder of Meredith Music Publications, Conductor Emeritus of the Bishop Ireton Symphonic Wind Ensemble (Alexandria, Virginia), Adjunct Professor of Music at The Catholic University of America, former chief editor for Music for Percussion, Inc., and past president of the Percussive Arts Society. He is the author of more than 20 highly acclaimed method books for percussion instruments, two supplementary band methods (co-author), solos and ensembles, and numerous articles for music journals.

B. Michael Williams teaches percussion at Winthrop University in Rock Hill, SC. He is an Associate Editor for *Percussive Notes* and composer of several works for hand drums, including "Four Solos for Frame Drums," "Bodhran Dance," "Another New Riq," "Tiriba Kan," and "Recital Suite for Djembe." For more information, visit www.bmichaelwilliams.com.

She-e Wu is Assistant Professor of Music at the Mason Gross School of the Arts at Rutgers University and a member of the Bob Becker Ensemble. Wu was a featured artist at the Journees de la Percussion in Paris, France and performed the marimba concerto of Eric Ewazen with Orchestre de la Garde Republicaine. She-e has also appeared at the Percussive Arts Society International Convention, the 4th National Percussion Convention of Spain, and many other major percussion festivals.

Zoro has toured and recorded with Lenny Kravitz, Bobby Brown, Frankie Valli and the Four Seasons, and many others. Voted No. 1 R&B drummer and clinician by *Modern Drummer* magazine, Zoro authored the award-winning and best-selling book and DVD package *The Commandments of R&B Drumming*, published by Alfred Publications. For more information visit www.zorothedrummer.com.

Functional Practicing

Kenny Aronoff

Functional Practicing is about accomplishing as much as possible every time you practice your instrument. It is about designing a practice routine that makes sure you practice the most important things every time you practice so that you are always prepared and sound good, whether it's for live performances, recordings, rehearsals with other musicians, or lessons with your teacher. It doesn't matter how many minutes or hours you practice; functional practicing involves organizing your practice time so you get the most out of the time you *are* practicing.

INGREDIENTS:
1. A drumset (but this recipe can be used for all musical instruments).
2. A metronome, drum machine, or something that keeps perfect time.
3. Manuscript paper or something to take notes on.
4. Lots of pencils and erasers
5. An iPod with headphones or speakers to hear the music you will be listening to.
6. A clock or watch to see how long you are practicing each segment of your practice routine.

Note: Not to be served with alcohol. Tea or water is recommended during the meal. Some protein, vegetables, and complex carbs are recommended one hour before beginning the meal.

You can apply this recipe to any time limit you have to practice. In other words, if you only have 30 minutes to practice, make this recipe work for 30 minutes. If you have two hours to practice, make it work for two hours.

SERVES:
All levels of players.

The Concept
Do you ever sit down to practice at your instrument, and wonder, "Where should I begin? Should I practice technique or work on music? Should I practice rudiments, beats, fills, double-bass-drum technique, four-way coordination, linear exercises, hand technique, foot technique, shuffles, grooves with and without fills? Should I focus on keeping time, my groove, my dynamics, my ability to solo, brush technique? Which book(s) or DVDs should I work out off? What style of music should I focus on—rock, hard rock, alternative rock, prog rock, modern rock, Latin, country, funk, R&B, hip-hop, jazz, fusion, African, Afro-Cuban, reggae, classical?"

There's no limit to what you can practice, and the tools we have today are endless. So I decided I had to be very organized about my approach to practicing in order to get the most out of it and get better as a drummer.

The basic concept of functional practicing is to practice what you need *right now, today*, so that you will sound great regardless of where you are playing. It doesn't matter what ability level you are at. It's better to play four things at A+ level, than to play 100 things at C- level.

For example, if you are playing in a band, you should design warm-up and technique exercises that are specifically related to the music you are playing with that band. Work on technique, beats, fills, grooves, time, and whatever else will make you sound better with *that* band playing *that* music. You can always improve on what you already know.

Another example is if you are taking lessons, make sure you practice your lesson before you start working on other techniques, songs, beats, fills etc. When you are practicing, *take care of the most important things first.*

The Recipe

1. Begin each practice session with warm-up exercises that focus on the type of technique you currently need to play and sound good. Use all four limbs at the same time, if possible, with every exercise you do, because when you are playing drumset you usually are using all four limbs simultaneously.

    Practice with a metronome or something that keeps perfect time to develop your ability to play with click tracks and loops. This is a functional approach to practicing. For example, when you warm up your hands (rudiments, rolls, etc.), include your feet even if you are just keeping simple time with them. When you do foot exercises, include your hands somehow.

    A. Warm-up exercises for the hands: Come up with hand exercises that use the same techniques you use when you play live gigs, or that you need for the type of music you are recording in the studio, or that you need for your private lessons. Practice things that will make you sound great at what you are doing every day on the drumset. Remember to include your feet as you are focusing on your hands.

    B. Foot exercises: Come up with foot exercises that use the same techniques you are using on your live gigs, or in the studio, or for your private lessons. Practice things that will make you sound great at what you are doing every day on the drumset. Work on double bass drum technique if you use that in your playing. Work on single, double, triple, and even quadruple bass drum groupings with beats and fills using your single bass drum pedal. Once again, include your hands while you focus on your feet so you are using all four limbs when you practice.

        This is functional practicing. The idea is to accomplish as much as possible while you are practicing.

2. Practice the beats you are playing every day in the band you play in, or for the lessons you're preparing for, or the music you are practicing, or any upcoming shows or gigs you have. Prepare for what you are about to do. Make sure you play those beats as well as possible before you start working on other beats.

3. Practice the fills you are playing in the band you play in, or the lessons you're preparing for, or the music you are practicing, or for any upcoming shows or gigs. Make sure you play those fills as well as possible before you start working on other fills.

4. Practice playing the beats and fills that you have been practicing together. Remember to practice all these exercises with a metronome or something that keeps perfect time.

5. Here is where you apply all the warm-up exercises, beats, and fills you practiced. In your iPod, put together a group of songs that you actually perform with the band you are in, or the songs you are preparing to play for an upcoming gig, audition, or lesson. Or put together a group of songs that has something to do with the techniques you were practicing. If you can write charts, notate the drum parts as detailed as possible; if you don't write charts, try to memorize the songs you are playing.

I personally write charts with every beat, fill, and anything else the original drummers did on the songs. It's a great learning experience to try and play songs perfectly. When I am getting ready for a tour and I want to build up my stamina and technique for a two-hour show, I will put a set of songs together on my iPod that is two hours long. I make very detailed charts and run through the set for two hours.

Dessert
After you have taken care of business and done your functional practicing, if you have more time, practice whatever you want to work on. Just have fun!

Inspired Practice

Anders Åstrand

We all know the importance of practicing technique and learning specific pieces of music note-for-note. But we often forget to practice in a way that exercises our creativity. The following recipe offers some ideas for practice sessions that inspire.

INGREDIENTS:
Marimba, vibraphone, drumset, and various percussion instruments
Recording tools: mini disc recorder and workstation, microphones, Alesis reverb unit
Video camera and digital camera on tripods
Music paper

SERVES:
Any musician at any level.

First course
Plan your practice for the next day (or week). For example: create a new setup (e.g., marimba, gongs, drums, cymbals) and work to play this setup as though it were a single instrument with many different "notes." Write some directions to use as a framework (e.g., different moods or rhythmic ideas).

Main course
Always record yourself when you practice. Take notes or record your comments while you are playing.

Also record yourself with a camera one or two minutes to check your body position; you will get quick information about shoulders, back, etc.

I use my reverb so I can play in different acoustics. For example, if I have a concert coming up in a church, I use one of the reverb settings to simulate the sound of a hall like that to get inspired.

Work with digital delays in different times, choruses, etc. This is great for inspiring creativity—and a great friend when you don't have other players around.

When possible, practice with other musicians and share ideas. Besides practicing with good friends who you play with often, also practice with combinations of instruments you don't usually perform with, such as vibraphone meets lute, or drumset meets mandolin.

Dessert
Listen back to your recorded "meal," take notes, and get inspired for your next practice session. ➤•

An Appetizing Rehearsal

John H. Beck

Percussionists have a particular concern when it comes to a rehearsal. It takes time to get the instruments in place before one can start the rehearsal. Trumpet players only need to get the mouthpiece and trumpet out of the case and they're ready play. Clarinet players put their instrument together, put a reed on, and start to play. Not so for percussionists. Getting ready to play can be a three-minute job or it can take a half-hour or more.

There is nothing more irritating to a conductor, or a whole orchestra or band, than having to wait for the percussionists to get ready. A recipe for an effective rehearsal is easy to follow and the results are excellent.

INGREDIENTS:
Music
Instruments
Sticks
Mallets
Pencil
Good attitude
Focused eye
If anything is missing, the rehearsal will surely fail.

SERVES:
One to one-hundred or more.

According to Webster, a rehearsal is "a private performance or practice session preparatory to a public appearance." An appetizer "stimulates the appetite and is usually served before a meal." Therefore, the rehearsal leading to a public performance is like the appetizer that comes before the dinner.

Percussionists must be keenly aware that in order for the rehearsal to start on time, they must get to the rehearsal in enough time to have the instruments ready for the downbeat. This amount of time is directly proportionate to the distance from the percussion storage area to the stage and the number of instruments needed (one snare drum, brief time; multiple-percussion setups, lots of time). Someone must also organize the distribution of instruments among the players. In a symphony orchestra, this is the Principal Percussionist's job. Without organization, disaster will surely prevail.

Don't show up without the music. It's a good idea to get the music well in advance of the first rehearsal so the time element can be figured out. Study the music and come up with a plan that enables you to be ready on time. If there is an instrument you do not have, figure out how you are going to get it or think of a substitute instrument you have that will work until the correct one can be obtained. It's always good to discuss this with the conductor ahead of time.

Have all the sticks and mallets you need to properly play the part. Have alternate sticks and mallets in case, after hearing the part in context with the band or orchestra, there might be a better choice.

Don't show up without a pencil. Mark the part carefully as you rehearse it. The conductor may ask for a particular musical accent, phrase, or *ritard*, and you think you will remember it, but chances are you won't, so mark it at that moment. I have never been impressed when a student or professional player shows me a clean percussion part that has no markings. In the heat of a concert, these little marks may prevent mistakes.

A good attitude and a focused eye need special mention, as they are the personal, non-musical elements that make a rehearsal effective. They are also attitudes that affect every musician—not just percussionists. Arriving at the rehearsal with the following attitudes will surely prove negative to an effective rehearsal: I don't like this conductor; I hate rehearsing in this auditorium; this orchestra/band is not very good. Arrive with a positive attitude and things will go much better.

Sometimes personal problems are taken into a rehearsal, and concentrating on the music is difficult. You must learn to keep personal problems off the stage and deal with them after the rehearsal or concert.

A focused eye on the conductor is helps ensure good music-making and a comfortable working relationship between you and the conductor. Every entrance should be made with an eye on the conductor. The conductor will appreciate it, and your comfort level will be much higher.

When all ingredients are properly added to the rehearsal it will lead to a fine performance, just as a good appetizer leads to an enjoyable dinner. ➤●

Southern Italian Tambourine Pizzica

Alessandra Belloni

An introduction for beginners and professionals to a very energetic tambourine technique from Southern Italy, this recipe will enable students, professional drummers, and the female drumming community to learn a new style of tambourine, which has a healing and a stress-release effect.

The *tarantella* is one of the most powerful healing dances in the world, and one of the most ancient music and dance therapies still practiced today. The *pizzica* ("bite," referring to the mythical bite of the tarantula) is the fastest of all the tarantella, and the accents are very strong and usually played with the thumb.

INGREDIENTS:
Recommended: Remo Alessandra Belloni Signature series red tamburello (one row of jingles) or the white Pizzica tambourine (double row of jingles). You can try other tambourines that are 12 inches wide, but they must be very light. Riqs or tars are not recommended.
Relaxed wrists.
Strong thumb.

SERVES:
Fast 6/8 and 12/8 rhythms.

Preparation
Let's imagine we are cooking a very special pizza. The Italian tambourine is round as a pizza, 12 to 16 inches wide. The skin is the same color as the dough, and it must be tight to make a good sound. Like the dough, you have to tighten the skin and stretch it to make it fit into the frame (which is like the sift or strainer used to plant the wheat seeds, from which they make the flour for the dough).

Playing position
The Southern Italian tambourine is usually played by putting the left hand all the way through the handle, holding the drum slanted and up with the wrist (which moves continuously), and hitting the skin with the palm and fingertips of the right hand. If you are left handed, the right hand holds the tambourine and you play with the left.

The Sauce
To make a good "sauce" you have to play hard, hitting all the different accents, using your whole hand, thumb, the back of your hand, and fingertips. Stirring the sauce is the movement of the playing hand, starting with the thumb striking the center of the skin, rotating your hand up, then going down with the fingertips to play. The more relaxed

you are when you "stir" the rhythm, the easier it becomes, the better it sounds, and the faster you can play.

The holding arm is the fire that cooks the pizza. Continuously moving in side motions and up and down, it keeps the "fire" of the rhythm, preventing your arm from getting tired, and keeping a steady rhythm, thus developing the stamina needed for playing many hours.

The wrist of the holding hand moves continuously, allowing the jingles to make a rhythmic sound according to the beats played by the playing hand, which hits the skin rotating off the thumb, with a very loose wrist, going up with the palm of the hand, creating a natural bounce, then going down with the fingertips in the center of the skin. This rotating motion of the hand divided into three movements makes the notes of the triplet, played up towards the jingles, to create a loud and repetitive 6/8 or 12/8 for the *pizzica tarantata* style. The accents, which have to be very strong, are executed with the thumb, which is used like a drumstick.

Cooking Time

The rhythm played on the tambourine is a very fast, obsessive 6/8 or 12/8 with specific accents played on the upbeat, called *battuta in levare*, and each cycle of the accents is a phrase of the song. The accents vary also according to the singing and the phrases of the violin or the accordion.

The main difficulty of the recipe consists in balancing the instrument between the two hands, so that the movement of the drum will not tire only one arm. By following the steps of wrist relaxation and arm movement you will develop the stamina, as the *pizzica* is usually played for many hours during a ritual.

Flavors

The different flavors are the different styles and slaps: dums, thumb, and fingertip sounds for the tarantella or *pizzica tarantata*.

First note of the triplet: With a very loose wrist on the playing hand, hit the center of the skin of the tambourine very loud and strong with the side of your thumb.

Second note: Rotate your hand up, hitting the edge of the tambourine with the back of your hand as the tambourine falls loosely on your hand to create the bounce.

Third note: Move your hand straight down to hit the center of the tambourine with your fingertips closed. At the same time, move the wrist of the holding hand, keeping the tambourine at waist level with your hand through the handle, moving the wrist in as the elbow goes out, and moving the elbow in as the wrist goes out. This motion with a loose wrist of the holding hand creates a louder sound of the jingles, which is really important to create a sound that is trance inducing.

Repeat this exercise eight times.

Accents on a 6/8 triplet rhythm

ta = thumb	ra = rotation of the hand, with back of the hand hitting the edge of the tambourine.
TA = accented thumb.	tum = fingertips closed, going down hitting the center of the skin.

In this style the accents are played by the thumb. A typical tarantella accent pattern is 1, 1, 1 2, 1.

TA ra tum ta ra tum TA ra tum ta ra tum TA ra tum TA ra tum TA ra tum ta ra tum

Repeat this exercise 16 times, keeping both wrists relaxed and very loose, moving your elbow in and out, accompanying the tambourine in a natural bounce.

When your wrist feels ready for more speed and the thumb feels ready for stronger accents, you can speed up and practice the *pizzica* accents at a faster speed (the correct metronome tempo is 170).

Keep your upper body relaxed. The more you move your body the easier it becomes to play faster triplets. Think of it as a drumming dance.

If you can practice this rhythm for 30 minutes without getting tired, you have put the right ingredients and cooked the right "pizza," meaning you are playing the *pizzica*!

Performance technique
The main skill of the tambourine player is to combine the technique with stamina with great physical strength, since the players go on for six or seven hours nonstop, without ever loosing the beat. The tambourine supports the violin and the voice, and the skill of the drummer is the ability to follow the musicians and singers in the variations.

You can develop stamina by practicing as well as through relaxation of the wrists.

There are many ways of playing the *tamburello*, and each player develops his or her own technique, using the movement of the whole body. I have certainly developed my own technique through the years, and you can do the same when you become more relaxed and familiar with this technique.

Historical Background
The Italian tambourine or *tamburello* is an ancient musical instrument connected to rituals often associated with women, dating back to ancient Egyptian and Sumerian cultures. In Magna Graecia (now Southern Italy) and the Middle East, women used frame drums for rituals honoring the Moon Goddess. In Rome, both men and women played the tambourine in rituals honoring Dionysus and Cybele (the Black Goddess of the earth). Many times priestesses used frame drums and tambourines in the Mysteries in honor of the Earth Goddess. In the South of Italy the tradition of the tambourine used in healing ceremonies, the rites of Dionysus, and honoring the Great Mother has never died.

The *tamburello* is still used today in Italy to accompany folk dances such as *tarantella*, *saltarello*, and the *tammorriata* in honor of the Black Madonna. This particular ritual is a continuation of the rites in honor of Cybele.

In Puglia the instrument is used for the music and trance dance therapy called *pizzica tarantata*, which is used to cure the mythical bite of the tarantula. *Pizzica* literally means "bite," a reference to the "bite of love."

This dance became popular as "Tarantella," and it was actually a healing trance dance of purification performed traditionally mainly by women, who played the "cure" on large tambourines with a double row of jingles to heal the afflicted women (*tarantate*), who fell into a hypnotic state of mind. They suffered from a mental disorder known as *tarantismo*, a form of depression usually caused by unrequited love and repression of erotic desires. They felt trapped in the spider web of the society, and the dance and rhythm helped free them from their imaginary spider web.

The women were indeed possessed by the spider, and the Tarantella became known as a musical exorcism which was performed for three days and three nights during the time of the summer solstice.

Playing with Other Instruments

Ivana Bilic

I have always enjoyed playing with other people. For me, the presence of another musical personality gives an extra impulse to my imagination. Some of the most useful remarks that I've received concerning my playing were given by musicians who were not percussionists. When you play with a fellow percussionist you have similar problems and the same vocabulary. Playing with other instruments can sometimes test the limits of your technical and expressive possibilities—and your patience.

INGREDIENTS:
A pair of good ears
Some fresh ideas
Open mind
Patience

SERVES:
Any percussionist at any level

Prepare as much as possible before you start to cook something with your oboe or viola friend. And please, listen. Go to concerts peformed by other instrumentalists and singers.

When you come to the rehearsal, nobody will talk to you about the sticking of a particular passage, the advantages of this or that grip, the mallets you are using, and so on. You will dicuss such issues as articulation, balance/dynamics, intonation, and, of course, *music*.

Percussion instruments in general have a very immediate attack and, except for the timpani, no possibility to change the pitch. Balancing the intonation can sometimes be a little tricky. It is very important to consider it even if you are playing on instruments with no determined pitch. Still, by changing the quality of the sound you can slightly change the pitch, too.

Forte or *piano* are not absolute categories. What do *forte* or *legato* or *strepitoso* mean for a flute and what do they mean for timpani? You will need all the fresh ideas about mallet choice, articulation, and dynamics you can come with.

You can produce so many different sounds if you really start to use your ears. No matter how different, if treated by a master composer there are practically no instruments that can't play together.

All these experiences playing with other instruments are very rewarding, and when you come back to practice a percussion piece, you will have a completely new view on it. ➤

Creative Music-Making and the Drumset Player

Bob Breithaupt

For years, a centerpiece of drumset study has been the coordination book or, as it is often somewhat incorrectly referred to, the "independence" book. In fact, a standard pedagogical approach has evolved around introducing one coordination book after another, ultimately downplaying or eliminating the true essence of drumset: the aural learning process as it relates to style, coordination, and improvisation. This recipe will help to identify a strategy for incorporating a connection between aural recognition and physical application for drumset.

INGREDIENTS:
one drummer
one drumset
two ears
one brain
a CD player

SERVES:
The contemporary drumset teacher and the dedicated student of any age.

Drumset coordination is a critical element in the effective realization of a musical result on the instrument, though "coordinating" oneself on the drumset goes far beyond being able to play at one rate with one limb while playing a different rate with another. Following are practical factors that relate to the most fundamental issues of coordination:

Balance
Striking a drum with a two-inch stroke and a ride cymbal with a ten-inch stroke and hoping for a simultaneous sound to occur is unreasonable—and will not lead to even, balanced sounds between limbs. Therefore, working toward coordination that sounds even and balanced without balanced stokes, heights, and motions is next to impossible. This concept is so simple to understand when playing a musical passage on marimba or balancing a group of players, but is seldom applied on the drumset. **Finished product:** Listen and watch for evenness and the subsequent balanced sounds in basic coordination exercises.

Sing Out!
Use that wonderful free instrument that we all have, our voice, to assist us in opening the doors to a more creative approach. Any pattern or "groove" should be able to be sung—or at least replicated through the use of your voice. The act of singing a pattern will cause you to internalize it and allow for an immediate connection between the ears, voice, and limbs. You may have noticed that the eyes were not a part of this equation, as they are *not* required,

and sometimes not desired for the pattern, groove, or style to be learned through reading it. **Finished product:** The more you have the sound "inside" you, the more adaptable it can be to tempo, dynamics, and other, more subtle, changes.

Free Patterns and Materials!

The creation of ideas and materials for coordination and improvisation can come from you, not from a book. As simple a process as singing a two-bar phrase can provide a myriad of options for improvisation, style variation, or new grooves. As an example, you can sing a simple, swing-style rhythmic line, which will then serve as material for coordination and/or comping exercises; ideas are only as limited as your imagination. **Finished product:** The line you sang can also be the departure point for an endless repertoire of musical ideas applied to the drumset.

Open Up the Spice Cabinet

As an instructor, don't rely on the "same-old/same-old" approach to presenting your lessons; challenge yourself and your students. And most important, remember that the drummer is an improviser, orchestrator, and a composer—not a metronome. **Finished product:** While steady time is a critical element of effective performing, the ability to respond to others and adjust a basic time feel through a broad, confident approach to style is critical.

Fill Up the Cupboard For the Future

Much like stocking up the cupboard, obtaining a diverse set of musical ingredients through listening and playing will pay dividends for the future. While there is greater access today to material through the Internet and other sources, the mass media does not highlight the broad spectrum of musical styles that it once did; the young player must seek them out. Through listening, downloading, viewing, etc., a musician can obtain an incredible set of inspirations. **Finished product:** These inspirations can translate into materials from which ideas and creativity can flow, resulting in a musician who is infinitely more well-rounded than ever before. ➤●

Feeding the Imagination

Bill Bruford

Most musicians work within a comfort zone, determined in part by what it is they think they can do well, and in part by a series of real or imagined "rules." Nothing unreasonable about that, but big leaps forward can occasionally be achieved by deliberately placing yourself in a situation that's new to you. This can be as simple as limiting the instruments you use on a given piece, or as scary as working in a style with which you are almost completely unfamiliar. The aim is to hear and watch yourself react "outside of the box." You'll need to trust that your innate musicality will come up with something, and that something may surprise you with its appropriateness (Where did that come from?). You'll need to remember that nothing you are or are not doing is as critical to the outsiders, your colleagues, as it is to you, especially if you haven't told them you are hopelessly out of your depth.

INGREDIENTS:
3 heaping tablespoons of imagination (sometimes hard to find in your local supermarket)
2 pints of active listening (across all genres)
16 oz. of fearlessness
1 lemon, sliced

SERVES:
All creative musicians.

Recipe
Mix the imagination and active listening for several months. Be sure to avoid all contact with prejudice. Let sit. Put in oven and bake to produce a thick skin of about three inches deep, impervious to humiliation. Spoon in the fearlessness for courage. Add sliced lemon to taste. Will deliver a zesty tang and a sharp jolt to the system.

Mostly, with some minor variations, we bring a pre-prepared part, or template, to the music. That rhythm 'n' blues shuffle we've worked so hard on will suit nicely there; that Garibaldi funk thing will do for this song for the time being, until we can think of something more original, which we somehow never quite get around to. It's all workman like, but nothing to set the house on fire. As a creative musician you'll want to improve on that, and it will help immeasurably if you are in on the construction of the music from the ground floor up. When I started, band members sat around for hours in rehearsal rooms bashing out bits and pieces of ideas, riffs, sounds, hoping that someone would jump on something and breathe life into the spark. That's hopelessly old-fashioned and expensive to do now, but a rehearsal band, even if it never does any gigs, is a wonderful tool to have—a way to hear your wackiest ideas realized.

What you are looking for here is a safe environment in which to experiment, to imagine the unimaginable, and then to feed the results back into your more regular work. If you hear yourself playing straight eighth notes on the hi-hat for a while, stop it, and put some holes in! If you play anything that continuously at me for more than a minute I'm going to stop listening, because my brain has said, "Uh-oh, nothing happening here. I'll listen to something else."

Usually, stopping doing something is at least twice as effective as doing something. When you've found out what I'm talking about, take that to your next session with another artist, and just do it until you're told not to. Trust me, they'll love it (whatever "it" may be, at this point). From this, your confidence will leap forward—you and your idea survived; it really wasn't so bad!

It may be that your highly effective practice-room idea—smokin' as it is with just one drummer—needs amending to "sit" right with a whole band. Great: amend it! Don't give up. Persevere until it feels good. Now that you see that the easy part of this was a lot more difficult than you thought, and the difficult stuff was easier than you thought, you can make the appropriate changes next time.

Much of this has to do with the broad brush on the bigger picture. It's remarkably easy to get lost in the nuts and bolts of music making—the details—while failing to see that even if the details are, finally, all correct, the music isn't adding up to much. I wish I had ten bucks for every brilliant sounding demo I've heard: perfect sounding vocals on an immaculate recording on a state-of-the-art home-recording system, drums good enough to eat, latest plug-ins and outboard effects all ticking away nicely, everything in time and ticketyboo, but completely devoid of the slightest whiff of anything original. I'd rather have a good idea poorly played than a terrible idea well executed, but it should be possible to have strong ideas well played. There is more to this music thing than just "getting it right"—what Frank Zappa called "industrial correctness." I'm sure when Pink Floyd added "found sound" and industrial noise into their tracks, influenced by the "musique concrète" movement, or the Beatles added a sitar, or King Crimson used two guitarists, but *neither would play any chords, only single lines,* the people who were thinking this stuff up weren't thinking about industrial correctness. No one is expecting you to be wholly original—if you were, we'd probably not recognize it as music—but it may be possible to stir up and mix the ingredients in an original way.

Same with our individual instrument, in this case the drumkit, and how we perceive its role and function in the music. Electronic drums in jazz? Are you out of you mind? I don't know, but let's find out. A rock group without cymbals or hi-hats? Why? I don't know, but let's see what happens. Two drummers hammering away in different meters? But what if half the audience dances to one and the other half dances to the other? It'll probably be great!

It's ironic that the ever greater availability of music we have, the less anyone seems to listen to it. The cheaper it gets, the less anyone values it. The ever-increasing options on what we can do with a drumset seem to produce a current crop of rock drummers all doing roughly the same thing in roughly the same tempo, and certainly in the same time-signature. *And, really, they don't have to.* The slightest departure from convention—playing the bridge on the toms, for example—is jumped on by every other group in the same field, and appears instantly on MTV like a rash overnight. It's extraordinary the extent to which, when we play, we conform to some prescribed notion of what it is that a drummer "should" do.

When I started, the notion of keeping "steady" clock-time, now evidently a matter of life or death, wasn't given much of a premium. Progressive rock groups like Yes and King Crimson moved in "orchestral time," as if the drummer were also the conductor. Tempi picked up here and slowed there according to the demands of the music. What felt right was right. Then Roger Linn invented his famous drum machine, and everything was suddenly measured according to the clock, and studios were full of tyrannical producers stopping the drummer because he had a three millisecond flam with his kick drum as measured against the click; "Look, see? Computer says so, right here."

Before machines, the way a drummer approached the time was as much a part of his makeup and identity as his sound. The jazz guys tended to rush like crazy. Tony Williams was well on top of the beat. Elvin stretched time like it was bubblegum. Steve Gadd played jazz with Chick Corea in an unusually steady tempo gained from years playing with clicks in studios.

If you assume a drummer's function is to "keep time," then the convention that a drummer starts at the beginning of a tune and plays all the way though makes sense. If, however, you step back a bit and consider keeping time to be only one of several functions that the drummer may have, then it may be the guitarists who assign themselves the function of keeping the continuum going, and the drummer who stops, starts, adds and removes his weight, comments on proceedings, and generally plays havoc with light and shade. In the King Crimson of the 1980s in which I served, it was usually the guitarists who were first and last to be heard on the track, often unaccompanied by any percussion for short or long passages. Try to find out what you are doing with that darn drumkit thing, and the rest will fall naturally into place.

I was once paid quite well for contributing silence to a track. Admittedly, it was a collective improvisation and a live recording, but my contribution of steady silence affected the course of this instantaneous composition as surely as if I had blasted forth with a juddering onslaught of pneumatic bass drums and machine-gun snare. The music needed no percussion, so I contributed none. I was credited, therefore, with co-composer rights and remunerated accordingly. Quite right, too.

Providing what the music requires—or at least giving it a chance to tell you what it requires rather than what you require—is an underused strategy. You exist to serve the music, the music doesn't exist to serve you. If the music demands silence, that's what you provide. If it wants a log-drum and three bass drums, then that's what you provide. The brilliant Terry Bozzio is hearing a certain kind of music in his head which can only be realized with the gargantuan drum setup he uses. Trust me, he wouldn't be lugging that lot around unless the music demanded it!

The first technique you will need is imagination, and then an ability to listen actively, imaginatively, and without prejudice. Your primary function is to produce some music; it's marketing is only a secondary function. All the creative musicians realize this. Try to imagine the complete composition without your drums, without any drums, and then build it up from there on in. I have always tried to produce absolutely tune-specific parts that will only apply or be useable on that one tune, and that one tune only. Ideally the rhythmic part should be entirely listenable and self-sustaining on its own as a little rhythmic composition, were the rest of the band to stop playing.

Ideas? The great drummer of Soft Machine, Robert Wyatt, so the story goes, had his tech set his drums up differently every night, just to keep him on his toes, and to make sure things sounded different. Try treating the drums with mutes, cloths, specialist cymbals on the toms, or a tambourine on the snare drum. Try all those different sticks and mallets you can get these days. Plenty of hip guys are using "unbalanced" strikers—for example, a shaker-mallet in the left hand and a brush in the right, or a stick in the right and a mallet on the left, or similar unlikely combinations. This has an agreeably "random" effect of making the phrase less predictable.

Less is often more. Try confining yourself to an area of the kit only—say, for example, the woods (drums), and don't touch those metals (cymbals). Try doing a gig with just the Big Three (bass drum, hi-hat, and snare); that should focus the mind a little. The world won't stop; heck, the bass player probably won't notice, and the audience certainly won't. You see, they care about you and your problems a whole lot less than you think they do, and that's good news! Means you are a whole lot more free than you thought you were to come up with interesting, fresh and useable ideas—and no excuses! ➞●

Interpretation and Expression

Michael Burritt

How do I make educated decisions in regard to the interpretation of a given piece of music? Is there a correct or accepted interpretation? Is it okay for me to bring my own musical ideas and personality to the work? Once I develop my interpretation, how can I become more expressive in my performance? Is my performance effectively communicating my interpretive and expressive ideas?

These are questions I hear from students quite often. They are excellent and valid questions, and truly some of the most difficult areas of music to teach. Let's see if we can come up with some concrete ways to tackle these issues.

INGREDIENTS:
An eagerness to learn and an inquisitive personality
A willingness to try new ideas
A set of open ears
A spirit of experimentation

SERVES:
All musicians

Interpretation
When learning any piece of music I believe it is absolutely essential to study all aspects of the work. It is common to learn the notes, dynamics, and tempo indications and then go about the task of perfecting the piece technically and musically. What I find often missing is what I call the "investigative process." This process is tremendously important to making good, educated decisions in regard to interpretation.

The investigative process should include researching the background of the work. What period does the work come from in overall music history as well as within the specific composer's output? For what occasion and for whom was the piece written? Are there other works to listen to and study by the composer that can help you have a better understanding of the intent of the piece? Not only will this process bring you closer to the music you're working on but it will also enhance your overall knowledge of music/percussion history.

The second part of this investigative process is a formal and theoretical analysis of the music. I'm not suggesting that you write a theory paper about the piece (although that's not a bad idea!). What I am referring to is a basic understanding of the melodic, harmonic, motivic development and overall form of the work. Is the piece in minor or major? Is it modal or twelve-tone? What key areas does the work move through and what relevance do these key areas have in relation to each other? Is the piece in sonata from, theme and variations, rondo, or possibly through-composed?

Think of it like a road map. In order to truly understand how to get from one place to another, it's always helpful to have a good sense of what your route looks like from above. This is also true in music. Your analysis should ultimately provide you with a map outlining the musical journey of the piece.

Finally, listen to recordings of the work by other percussionists or marimbists, if available. If it is a transcription of a piece originally written for another instrument, listen to recordings of the piece performed on its intended medium. You can learn a tremendous amount from hearing other musicians' interpretation, especially those outside of percussion.

Remember, the degree to which you understand the music can and will have a direct effect on the integrity of your interpretation.

Expression

Developing the expressive qualities of our playing is a life-long process. I find that it changes quite often as my musical ideals and life experiences grow. This is also one of the most challenging areas of music making to impart on your students. All we can do as educators is to impart some tools and steer students in a direction that enables each individual to find his or her own musical voice. Here are some ways that help me and my students move toward a more expressive performance.

Make it personal! What are you thinking about when you play a given work? Is there a different mood, color, or person you reflect on as you play different sections of the piece? If not, then go about the task of assigning an emotion or even a standard musical designation such as *dolce* or *cantabile* to help you clarify the different sections or movements of the piece. Is it "energetic" or "romantic"? Is it rounded or angular? Intense or joyous? You decide!

Once you have made some of these decisions, implement them in an extreme way. Why extreme? Whenever I try a new food, I take a big bite in order to fully experience the new taste and to know whether or not I like it. Maybe even several big bites! I believe the same thing to be true of music making. Try the new musical ideas in a way that makes a significant impact on the passage and gives you a true sense of the new "flavor." Then decide if you like it. If not, try a more subtle version of the change, continuing until you're satisfied.

I also encourage my students to sing passages. This is a wonderful way to hear a true sense of line or phrase in a given passage. I often do this in my teaching and my personal practice. This forces you to pull the phrase away the instrument and helps you, as the performer, to hear it as a line unto itself. How would a cellist, pianist, or clarinetist play the line? These are questions we should ask ourselves often. We need to think (and hear) more like musicians and less like percussionists.

Once you have tried singing the phrase or line, try it on your instrument. Decide if your playing reflects the line that you sang. I think you'll be surprised at how much this changes the way you play a passage. Singing is not only important for keyboard percussion; you can apply this to rhythmic phrasing on snare drum and timpani as well. Line is certainly not something exclusive to melodic instruments.

Improvising is another fun way to learn to play with more intuitive expression. Many people are intimidated by the idea of improvising. You don't have to be a great jazz musician to improvise. This can be as simple as improvising on the rhythms in a given piece or etude. Improvising on the scale, modality, or melodic patterns of a piece will help you become better connected with the language of the work. It's also a fantastic way to get to know your instrument better and a great way to warm up. Improvising was the launching pad for me to begin composing. You never know where it might lead you.

A final suggestion is to audio and video record your practicing. This will help you evaluate your performance from a more objective point of view. I am amazed at how much I learn from any recording of my performances or practice sessions. I can be either pleasantly surprised or rudely awakened. I prefer the first but I learn much more from the latter.

The expressive and interpretive qualities of our playing are the most subjective and personal ones. It could also be said that these are the most important qualities, for it is through these areas that we forge and develop our musical voice or personality. And it is through these areas that our musicianship will ultimately be judged. ➝●

Cooking In Time

Bill Cahn

If you are living in a "24/7" world of commitments and activities, you may have found that the amount of time available for the preparation of music for studio lessons and/or concert performances is very limited. In such a scenario it is important that any available practice time be used as efficiently as possible in order to get maximum results. A good recipe for efficient practice is simply this: *Use practice time mainly to work on the problem areas—not on the sections that don't need it.* In order to accomplish this, it is necessary to pose self-directed questions and then find answers that work. In essence, this is self-learning/teaching.

INGREDIENTS:

1. Available time: Try to schedule fixed practice time periods of 60 to 120 minutes, and whenever possible use shorter lengths of practice time, too. To avoid mental fatigue, it's advisable to take a break from practicing for at least an hour or more after 120 minutes.

2. Available instruments: If practicing a multiple-percussion piece, try, of course, to maintain the setup in place so that practice time is not lost locating and setting up instruments. If that's not possible, extra setup time will have to be factored in to the practice plan.

3. A practice plan with specific goal(s): A sample practice plan is given below. Essentially, the plan involves focusing practice time on identifying and addressing specific musical problems.

4. The ability to ask (and answer) the right questions: Asking the right questions involves good listening and self assessment. Start each practice session with these two questions: What can be accomplished in the amount of practice time available? What specific problem(s) will this practice session address?

5. Helpful equipment: Meter or rhythm problems may require the use of a metronome. A recording device with mic and earphones (audiocassette, CD, mini-disc, or a computer/ laptop with software like *Garage Band*) can be a valuable resource in identifying problems and assessing progress.

SERVES:

The practice plan that follows is one that can be useful to any musician, whether student, amateur, or professional.

The Practice Plan (Recipe)

The recipe for efficient practicing is simple: *Use practice time mainly to work on the problem areas—not on sections that don't need it.* This recipe involves having the ability to ask oneself the right questions at the right time and then to come up with good answers. The ultimate goal of any practicing is to internalize the music—to sort out and then express the relationships between the printed page and one's own motions, emotions, intuitions, and inner truths.

There are only a few basic steps in a good practice plan, assuming that excessive muscle tension is avoided and that the player's body is generally relaxed.

STEP 1. Get a Sense of the Big Picture

At the beginning of every session, play through the entire piece/etude/exercise once. Listen while playing. If possible, record yourself playing, because listening to the playback while disengaged from playing more clearly points out the problem areas.

STEP 2. Identify the Problems

Depending on which of the phases of practice a work-in-progress is at, ask and then answer appropriate questions. Phase 1 is practicing to learn the notes. In this phase certain passages in the music will normally be easy to play through, while other passages are difficult. Of course, the difficult sections will be easy to identify, but it is important to ask the following questions even for the easy sections.

- Were muscles relaxed? Is there body tension anywhere?
- What was heard or noticed? Were the notes, tempos, dynamics, tone correct?
- Were the stickings the most efficient for each note?
- What was liked/disliked about what was heard? Where were the specific problem spots?

In Phase 2 of practicing, the notes are organized into phrases/sections.

- Are muscles relaxed? Is there body tension anywhere?
- What was heard or noticed? Were the notes, phrases, shapes correct?
- Do the phrases make sense rhythmically/dynamically/tonally?
- What was liked/disliked about what was heard? Where were the specific problem spots?

In Phase 3, practicing focuses "flow"—a sense of spontaneity in presentation in which musical expression is deep, immediate, effortless, and without thought.

- Were muscles relaxed? Is there body tension anywhere?
- What was heard or noticed?
- What was liked/disliked about what was heard? Where were the specific problem spots?

STEP 3. Address the Problems Identified

Work on each identified problem separately in the order of occurrence; don't waste time practicing passages that can already be played.

Start again from the beginning of the music and play up to and through the first problem area. Then work only on the problem area until it can be played three times in a row as desired.

Start again from the beginning of the music and play up to and through the corrected area. If the problem remains, work again only on the problem area until it can be played three times in a row as desired.

When the problem area has been played through from the beginning as desired, go on to the next problem spot and then repeat this step.

STEP 4. Start Again at the Beginning of the Music and Play Through the Piece
This final step will return the player to the big picture and identify problem areas for the next practice session.

That's all there is to it! There's no magic. Having successful practice habits is an essential part of being a successful musician. Granted, practice is frequently understood as being tiresome, repetitive, and mindless. However, while practicing is certainly not a substitute for real music-making, which is just about the most fulfilling pursuit one can have, practice is a necessary part of achieving that fulfillment, and good practicing is simply a helpful way to get there sooner. ➨

For a Great Performance, Follow ALL the Directions

Jeff Calissi

In order for a recipe to yield a good outcome, one must follow the directions. A recipe doesn't necessarily need to be followed exactly as written; sometimes a handful or just a touch of a seasoning will do. However, in order for a dish to taste good, it's always best to follow each line of the recipe until the end.

Playing a piece written for marimba can be prepared in much the same way, such as following each line of the music and reading the "directions"—the information beyond the pitches and rhythms.

INGREDIENTS:
A marimba
An original piece or transcription
Two or four mallets

SERVES:
Anyone wishing to perform a piece of music on marimba.

Percussionists are generally adept at accurately reading rhythms and pitches; unfortunately, though, some ignore what takes place around those notes because of their experiences before learning a keyboard instrument. I believe most students enjoy playing marimba because of the combination of rhythm and melody; nevertheless, the true melodic shape of a piece can be unfamiliar to their ears because of their history of performing rhythmic figures on a non-melodic instrument such as snare drum. By the time many students are introduced to a mallet-keyboard instrument, it is usually after several years of performing exclusively in a rhythmic fashion.

Many times, I have encountered students who think they are fully prepared for a marimba lesson. After playing through the assignment, these students will usually turn to me for recognition of their completed task. Although the performance may be accurate in terms of rhythm, pitch, and sticking choice, there will likely be at least fifty percent of the "directions" the students will have not understood, or even read, during their preparation.

When practicing for a lesson, students oftentimes play the correct pitches and rhythms, but not the shape of the phrases, and they ignore much of the dynamic and melodic content. I often find myself saying "play the music, not just the notes," because in initial stages of practice, percussion students often do not see a piece as comprising melody, harmony, and timbre. I will tell them to "follow all of the composer's directions" in order to first get a basic outline, and then continue in the same manner through each line of music. Thus, students should be shown there are several "directions" between and around the rhythms, pitches, and meter changes they understand so well.

In order to realize all of what composers intend in their music, think of how a non-percussionist would perform the work. This concept can be foreign to percussion students, so I suggest asking them to show the piece to friends who are a vocalists or who play other instruments in order to get their impression. By doing so, percussion students will recognize that wind and brass players and vocalists are cognizant of issues percussionists largely do not see, such as phrasing, listening, and understanding the construction and the direction of the music.

Many original marimba pieces suffer from a lack of phrase markings. Therefore, ask the students to sing the melody or think of how a woodwind or brass player would play it. Have them pay close attention to the amount of air they are using while singing. This will have an affect on their listening skills in terms of how long or short a phrase may be.

The ability to sustain sound on a marimba is akin to other instruments, but the natural decay of the marimba bar is also proportionate to the amount of air one uses for a wind or brass instrument. In addition to playing on the proper area of the bar, students should also consider the correct amount of sustain if someone were to play a similar passage, measure, or note on an instrument other than a marimba. This especially is true for transcriptions, as it affects the decision to add rolls and other means of sustain.

Most often, the shape and contour of an entire work is comparable to a story with a rising action, a climax or high point, and a falling action. Many pieces written for today's percussionists includes such structure, but percussion students may not be hearing what another instrumentalist or vocalist would hear and play. So, by breaking down the phrases into playable parts for an instrument that requires breathing, the marimba student can look at the piece from a wider angle and locate and perform the high and low points and overall direction of a piece appropriately.

When students follow all the directions in a piece of music, they will understand the information beyond rhythm, pitch, and meter. As the tempo increases and muscle memory begins to work, students can then add their own interpretation and, in turn, a performance will reveal itself to the player and, ultimately, the audience. Too many times, percussionists become concerned with the kinesthetic nature of performance and the idiomatic position of the notes in their hands, and fail to think about what the composer truly wishes for in terms of melody and the overall shape of a piece. If *all* the "directions" are followed, the composer's "recipe" will yield a great performance. ➤●

Teaching Young Percussionists to Make Musical Choices

James Campbell

Percussion music for school band and orchestra often contains unclear instrumentation, puzzling orchestration, and confusing notation. Today's music educator must instruct young percussionists to make numerous choices when interpreting a piece of band or orchestra music, often providing much more detail than given by the composer or arranger who wrote the percussion parts in the first place. Because percussionists have a wide variety of instruments, mallets, and playing techniques available to them, each performer makes personal choices that greatly affect the overall sound of the ensemble.

INGREDIENTS:
3 fundamental roles
5 considerations for ensemble blend
4 articulations
dash of phrasing

SERVES:
Band and orchestra directors.

Consider this common occurrence: The percussion part calls for a cymbal, and the music is no more detailed than labeling the part "cymbal." However, we know that the sound of a cymbal can vary greatly with extremes in pitch, timbre, sustain, focus quality, and projection. Each cymbal has an individual sound that is determined by its diameter, weight, taper and thickness, profile shape, bell size, lathing and hammering technique, and the metal alloys used.

These construction techniques contribute to create a unique instrument that produces a specific quality of sound. With the wide variety of available instruments, some cymbals may not make an appropriate musical choice for the music to be performed. The percussionist and conductor must have a selection of instruments available to them, from which they choose which instrument makes the best sound for each musical situation.

This scenario happens more frequently than not. There are few standards in the percussion world, with new instruments, implements, and performance techniques being created all the time. It can be an overwhelming task for music educators, students, and even professional performers to keep up-to-date with all the resources that are available to them and to become familiar with the characteristic sound of every product and technique. Percussionists are unique in this respect, as other wind and string instrumentalists play instruments of standard construction and range with a commonly accepted performance practice.

3 Fundamental Roles

To make informed choices regarding musical interpretation, it is necessary to understand what role a particular instrument serves within a piece of music. Percussion instruments generally function in ensemble music in three fundamental ways, providing one or more of these functions, even at the same time, in a single phrase of music.

1. Melodic: play the primary lead voice, alone or with others, with a pitched instrument such as a keyboard or timpani, or imitate the melody with a non-pitched instrument such as a snare drum or woodblock.

2. Rhythmic/Harmonic: provide an accompaniment figure or provide pulse, alone or with others.

3. Coloristic: establish an atmosphere, provide a special effect, or emphasize a special moment, alone or with others.

5 Considerations for Ensemble Blend

As percussionists perform, they must listen keenly to the rest of the ensemble to determine their musical function and how they can best blend their sound with others who share their role. Encourage students to recognize with which instruments in the ensemble they play, and to imagine how they would support these parts. The students should imitate the contour and shape of the melodic line as they play along. The director must continually help the students develop an awareness of their musical role within the context of the ensemble.

Percussionists need access to a variety of instruments, implements, and performance techniques to select the most appropriate sound for each musical situation. Careful listening to the ensemble will help the percussionists choose the best sounding instrument, mallet, playing area, performance technique, and whether to dampen an instrument or allow it to resonate. Marked dynamic levels are often misleading because some percussion instruments naturally "speak" more strongly than others. Instruct students that dynamics are a relative indication, and that they must maintain constant awareness to achieve proper balance with their part.

Students can choose a unique texture or blend with other instruments when they consider:

1. Size: Choose the most appropriate size instrument for its pitch or tonality. Smaller instruments are generally brighter or have a higher pitch than large instruments of the same design.

2. Mallets: Choose appropriate implements. Soft, large-headed, and/or heavy mallets produce darker tones than hard, small-headed, and/or light mallets.

3. Playing area: Choose a specific striking area. Find the "sweet spot" on every instrument and use this as a reference point for achieving a full, vibrant tone. Aim for the correct playing area, not just the correct rhythm or note. Achieving consistency in the playing area is the first step toward playing with consistent, quality tone.

   A. Drums have three basic playing areas:

      • Center: lowest fundamental tone with minimal sustain.
      • Off-center: dark tone with sustain.
      • Edge: bright and thin tone with increased sustain.

B. Percussion keyboard instruments have three basic playing areas:

- Center of the bar: lowest fundamental tone with wide spectrum of overtones.
- Slightly off-center: dark tone with less pronounced overtones.
- Node: bright and thin tone.

4. Technique: Choose the correct performance technique for each instrument.

- Technique that emphasizes a firm grip, quick stroke, and a quick lift produces a bright and clear tone quality.
- Technique that emphasizes a relaxed grip, smooth stroke, and a natural lift produces a dark and vibrant tone quality.

5. Duration: Choose to dampen the instrument only when appropriate. Since percussion instruments have a natural decay, they should normally be allowed to sustain.

Percussionists should be flexible when interpreting note values and rests on percussion instruments. Composers and music editors often use rests to make percussion rhythms clearer and easier to read and do not always intend for a literal interpretation of note length.

- Let instruments vibrate freely if they're part of a melodic line or connect musical ideas.
- Dampen to imitate the note lengths of other instruments.
- Partial dampening can provide extra clarity to an active part. Place a mute or a cloth on an instrument to achieve a drier tone quality.
- Avoid "choking" a note by dampening too quickly. Allow the tone of the instrument to fully sound before dampening.

Articulation

Due to the natural decay characteristics of their instruments, percussion students may not accurately reproduce some written musical expressions and nuances such as breath marks, dynamic changes, articulations, and fermatas. Since wind players control the length and direction of their notes through the delivery of the air stream, they can control the shape of the entire note. Without the use of rolls or dampening, percussionists only have control of their attack characteristics. However, when percussionists are aware of all the expressive elements indicated in the music they can perform with a greater understanding of ensemble timing, articulation, and phrasing. Keep in mind that musical expression is most obvious on resonant percussion instruments.

Musical interpretation for a percussionist requires imagination and creativity. The main factors that contribute to tone quality are:

- Grip: how firmly or loosely the mallets are held.
- Volume: the height and/or speed from which the instrument is struck.
- Touch: the type of rebound off the instrument (upstroke) after striking it.

Discussing the differences between articulations and styles can be confusing to young instrumentalists—especially percussionists. In their early years, percussion students should begin to display awareness for nuances that will create a deeper understanding and communication of the following articulations:

Legato: A directive to perform a certain passage of a composition in a smooth, graceful, connected style.

- Maintain a light touch on the mallets at the grip point.
- Use a very fluid, full stroke with a natural rebound to create a legato attack.
- Allow the percussion instruments to sustain naturally.
- As the percussionist gains experience, softer implements and changes in playing area will enhance the legato articulation.

Staccato: A style of playing notes in a light, detached, and distinct manner.

- Maintain a firm touch on the mallets at the grip point.
- Use a very quick downstroke with a quick upstroke to create a staccato attack.
- As the percussionist gains experience, dampening, harder implements, and changes in playing area will enhance the staccato articulation. The use of "dead strokes" (leaving the mallets on the surface after striking) or quasi-dead strokes can be effective on some instruments.

Tenuto: A directive to perform a certain note or chord of a composition in a sustained manner for its full duration.

- Maintain a full, supportive grip in the entire hand.
- Use a slow downstroke with a small upstroke and added weight from the arm to create a tenuto attack.
- As the percussionist gains experience, softer implements and changes in the playing angle will enhance the tenuto articulation.

Marcato: A style of playing that means marked, accented, or stressed with a slight separation between notes.

- Maintain a full, supportive grip in the entire hand.
- Use a quick downstroke with a quick upstroke to create a marcato attack.
- As the percussionist gains experience, harder implements, partial dampening, and/or changes in playing area will enhance the marcato style.

Phrasing

Teach students to pay attention to the speed and shape of a melodic or rhythmic line and remember that every note goes to or comes from another note to help give direction to the music. In order to smooth out a melodic or rhythmic line, students often must emphasize the lower pitches of timpani, keyboard percussion, or multi-percussion setups in order to compensate for the greater projection qualities of the higher notes.

These general guidelines will help percussionists achieve greater expression:

- Sustained notes (rolls) should have some direction rather than simply maintaining the same volume. Repeated notes on the same pitch should also display some direction.
- A slight decrescendo from the first note to the last note of the phrase causes the notes to connect more as they ring into each other.
- Groups of notes or downbeats can be lightly accented or emphasized to keep the music buoyant and energetic. This nuance can be performed effectively by providing extra weight to the stroke of the notes that are emphasized.

Teaching student percussionists to become aware of their fundamental role within the ensemble, achieve the proper blend, perform with the proper articulation, and add a dash of phrasing will give them a recipe for success in the school music ensemble and beyond.

Exploring Interpretation Through Percussion Notation

Anthony J. Cirone

Percussionists have always been challenged as they try to discover a composer's musical intentions in orchestral and solo music. As timpani and percussion instruments were introduced in orchestral music, composers rarely used the same elements of music for winds and strings when writing parts for percussion. Important essential markings such as articulations, phrasing, and even note values never made it into timpani, snare drum, keyboard percussion, or accessory instrument parts. A percussionist also must deal with the lack of information provided for the exact instruments, sticks or mallets. The goal of this "recipe" is to enlighten performers, composers, and conductors in the art of interpreting percussion music.

INGREDIENTS:
Imagination
A Practical Guide to Percussion Terminology by Russ Girsberger (Meredith Music)
Cirone's Pocket Dictionary of Foreign Musical Terms by Anthony J. Cirone (Meredith Music Publications)

SERVES:
University students, professional performers, conductors, and composers.

Digest the following information over many years, adding a dash of Precision (technique), Sensitivity (dynamics), and Musicality (interpretation) along the way.

Let's start with a basic example of writing for timpani. The most common problem performers face when playing an instrument whose sound sustains after the pitch is stuck is that composers rarely indicate how long a particular note value should ring before muffling the sound or until it fades away. Many composers write only for "the moment of attack" on percussion instruments; they do not address the sustaining sound that results from the initial stroke.

The following excerpt, from the first movement of Beethoven's "Symphony No. 5," shows the French horn, trumpet, and timpani parts. We will begin our exploration here:

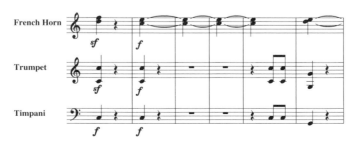

We see that the timpanist has the choice to muffle the timpani sound on the rests and play with the trumpets, or let the timpani sound ring and play with the French horns. If you study the full score, you'll notice all the winds and the contrabass play in a similar manner as the French horn. Most timpanists will follow the French horn part by muffling the first note on the second beat and letting the rest of the notes sustain. The reason for this is that the timpani sound will then resonate with the winds and basses and enrich the orchestral sound with its full, lush timbre.

Dvorak's "Symphony No. 9" ("Symphony from the New World") has one cymbal note in the entire work, and that note is a source of many interpretations. First of all, Dvorak tells us that this note is for "piatti," but he does not explain if he wants a suspended cymbal or a pair of crash cymbals. The Italian word "piatti" is similar to the English word "cymbal," which may denote either a suspended cymbal or crash cymbals. Decisions like these are usually left up to the player. Usually, most conductors are happy just to hear the sound of a cymbal in the correct place at the appropriate dynamic! The following excerpt is from this section:

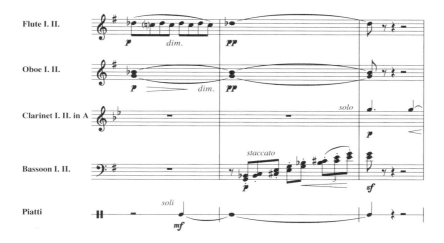

Since the cymbal entrance is at an *mf* dynamic without any reinforcement from the orchestra, the sound of a suspended cymbal with a yarn mallet blends well. Some players perform this note on a small pair of crash cymbals. Certain conductors have asked this to be played by sliding one crash cymbal against the inside of the other in order to produce a "swishing" sound. These decisions are all considered interpretations based on the player's experience, traditions within the percussion section, or the conductor's wishes.

It is interesting that Dvorak *did* notate exactly how long this sound should be sustained, which is very rare for classical composers. Whenever a part calls for "cymbals" with no other information, I suggest using the following general criteria for making a decision:

Use crash cymbals when:

1. There are many repeated notes in succession.

2. The cymbal note or notes are supported by unison entrances on the brass instruments.

3. The entrance is climatic and supported by the entire orchestra.

Use a suspended cymbal when:

1. There is an indication for a stick or mallet.

2. There are roll markings on the notes.

3. The cymbal entrance is written with a longer note value.

Many times a composer will write for a suspended cymbal, but not explain what type of stick or mallet to use. Also, we very rarely are told what size cymbal to use. These decisions all become part of the musician's interpretation.

An experienced percussionist will be able to determine whether to use a suspended cymbal or a pair of crash cymbals by the sound or character of the music at that point. The "swish" sound of a suspended cymbal blends well with softer and less rhythmic entrances, and the crash cymbals reinforce strong, powerful entrances. Of course, there are exceptions to this, but without any other information, it's a good benchmark.

Aaron Copland's "El Salón México" provides two interesting examples that require interpretation. First, we'll look at the snare drum part after rehearsal number 17.

Do we play this as abbreviated sixteenth notes or as rolls? In the abbreviated-note system, a quarter note with two slashes should be played as four sixteenth notes. Except for the two tied eighth-note rolls in the third and fourth measures (which actually have three slashes when counting the beam), this passage would then be played as notated below:

In order to decide on a definitive interpretation, listen to a recording of this music; it may make your decision a bit easier. This snare drum part is played with the trumpet and violins and it actually is a jazz "lick." I suggest using "crush" rolls. A more accurate notation is listed below:

Then there is the question of what type of snare drum to use for any given part (it is quite rare for a composer to indicate this). Here are some options:

1. Wood or metal shell

2. Wire, gut, or cable snares, or a combination of those

3. Plastic or calf heads

4. Shell depths ranging from four to six inches

It can be even more confusing when a composer writes for a tenor, field, or parade drum. I would like to pose a question: Which drums are played with snares "on" or "off"? Most composers don't know the answer to this question. A general rule is to use snares off for the tenor drum and snares on for field and parade drums. This gets even more complicated when the composer is writing in Italian, German, or French. I recommend *Cirone's Pocket Dictionary* or the *Practical Guide to Percussion Terminology* in helping with these decisions.

Now let's look at the woodblock part to "El Salón México" by Aaron Copland at rehearsal 13.

This seems like a very straight-forward part until we realize that some of the notes have a *staccato* marking, which, to a musician, is an indication to play the notes very short. Well, there is no shorter sound than striking a woodblock. Any note produced by the woodblock will sound very short with no perceivable resonance. What, then, did Copland have in mind? It only takes one hearing of the music to realize that Copland gave the woodblock player the exact rhythm of the melody. When woodwind, brass, or string players play a melody with a *staccato* indication, each one of those notes will not only sound "short" but will also have more of a presence than the notes without the *staccato* mark. This requires the percussionist to add a slight accent on each note.

Actually, adding any articulation to a non-resonating percussion instrument (snare drum, cowbell, temple block, etc.) adds a level of accent to the sound. The music example below indicates a series of different articulations. Starting with a normal note and then adding a *staccato*, *tenuto*, accent, and "wedge" accent, each articulation provides a slightly heavier emphasis to the note.

Copland does not suggest what type of stick or mallet to use on the woodblock. The normal choices are a wood stick (snare drum stick) or a medium-hard rubber mallet. There is quite a difference in the sounds between the wood stick and the rubber mallet. The snare drum stick produces a light "tick" sound while the rubber mallet produces a full, "round" sound. I suggest a rubber mallet for this part.

Interpreting percussion music can be very creative. We have so many choices to make regarding articulations, phrasing, note values, sticks, mallets, and the actual instruments to be used. When in doubt, it's always interesting to see if the conductor may have a suggestion!

For a more complete discussion of this subject, please see *On Musical Interpretation of Percussion Performance* by Anthony J. Cirone (Meredith Music Publications). ➤

Making It to the Top

F. Michael Combs

Before giving you the recipe for reaching the top, let's squelch all those notions we have heard so often and maybe even said ourselves:

"There are so many good players auditioning, I don't stand much of a chance."

"I probably won't win, but I will take this audition just to see what will happen."

"The odds of my getting the job are so slim I won't even try."

"The expectations of that college teaching position are more than I can come up to."

If your self-image is not as high as possible, that should be the first issue that needs attention—and it's not an issue that one short article can fix. However, the points here should help guide you toward establishing a realistic picture of your potential and capabilities. But don't think that having high expectations of yourself means that you don't need to constantly evaluate yourself and understand whatever shortcomings you may have.

INGREDIENTS:
1. Take a large amount of self esteem (if you are running short on that, it's okay; this article will help you).
2. Add a major dose of realistic expectations.
3. Stir in one well-done resume.
4. Add a pinch of good attitude with a clear vision of where you are going.
5. A large slice of a true evaluation of yourself.

Stir frequently over the course of your life.

SERVES:
Anyone facing an audition or job interview.

Attitude toward auditions
It's okay to consider your first one or two auditions a "testing of the waters" and an opportunity to learn how to take an audition. No matter what you have learned in the studio, you will never know how you are going to perform in a real audition until you actually do it. But you must quickly get out of the mode of taking auditions for "the experience" and "just to see how you will do" and get totally focused on *winning* that audition.

The odds of winning
Forget the odds. Someone has to win even if there are hundreds of excellent players auditioning. You have equal odds of winning—particularly in today's audition procedures that often

are behind a screen so that age, sex, and other physical features are not a factor. Don't let that long list of people auditioning diminish your focus or dampen your spirits. Otherwise, you will lose before you even audition. Also remember that the person playing just before you could deflate your ego by how fast he or she plays the "Porgy and Bess" excerpt, but your excellent cymbal playing and outstanding bass drum control might get *you* the job.

The expectations are too high

It's not advisable to waste your time auditioning for, or applying for, a position for which you are clearly not qualified. On the other hand, don't be turned off too quickly by job descriptions, especially for college teaching positions. At the collegiate level, the position description is usually written by non-percussion specialists (like the search committee or the department head), and it can be a wish list of qualifications that they hope to get in an applicant. Of the items on the list, there might be one or two qualifications that are not your strongest areas, but that could be outweighed by the many other special strengths you have.

This part of the recipe is to help you first get in a positive mindset and be realistic about your own capabilities. If you don't think you can win, the odds are that you will not. It's not a matter of luck but of ability.

What are you aiming for?

Most students, when asked about the highest position they would like to obtain, would probably say the principal percussion or timpani spot in one of the major orchestras, or teaching percussion in one of the finest percussion programs in a prestigious institution. Many others will say that getting to the top means getting the largest salary in the industry.

There is not an answer for you here, just good advice that setting your goals and establishing where and what your top position *really* is, is essential to everything else you do. And your top spot might be a very good orchestra that is in a particularly good location, or a college teaching position in a school where you can mold and develop your own program rather than having to live up to the previous teacher.

Creating the best resume

There is one document that can either get you in the door or do you in: your resume, sometimes called a vita or bio. The primary purpose of a resume is to convince the reader(s) that, from that huge stack of resumes, *you* should be invited to the interview. This is particularly true with college teaching jobs but can be true sometimes with professional playing positions.

Creating your resume by yourself is difficult because you see yourself in a totally different way than others see you. Don't try to do it alone; get professional help. That help can be your teacher or a professor with experience in this area. Since resumes in non-musical areas are so different than ours, there is little that a professional resume writer or even a computer program can provide for what you need. Many professional playing positions require a one-page resume that can be even more challenging to produce.

A special note to students doing this for the first time: Creating your first resume forces you to look at the big picture—to see the overview of your work. In doing so, you might note a shortcoming or an area that needs attention. College students can take advantage of this first experience at resume writing to realize the gaps they might want to fill in before they get out into the job market. Perhaps it would mean joining a professional organization or applying for a special award. The old saying "it will look good on your resume" will have more meaning as you develop this important document.

If you are just now creating your resume or have one that you need to update or review, there are five important points to keep in mind:

1. One resume will not fit all situations. You should have a basic resume that you will need to tailor for a playing position or reword for a college teaching position. That same resume will need to be adjusted if you want to use it as a bio in a program or on your Website.

2. Be honest. Don't pad or exaggerate. You would be a loser if someone discovered that information you included was not completely accurate.

3. Show yourself at your very best. Some accomplishments and awards might not seem so important to you, but listing them could make your resume more appealing and make a difference in the reader's impression.

4. Be specific. Include dates, locations, and anything that will make the information clear to the reader. Imagine someone reading your resume who is unfamiliar with your school and has never been to your city.

5. Make it very easy to read. In many situations, resume readers are going through a large stack of resumes looking for a way to reduce the number of applicants. Work with style, font, and other graphics (that is so easy with today's word processors) so that your resume is very eye-catching at first glance. But most importantly, be sure there is nothing in your resume that is a turn-off, such as political incorrectness. At an initial scanning, the reader must be blown away by how excellent you are; then, he or she will be motivated to read more of the details.

If you have not just a good but a *great* resume, that document will be a major support for you to make it to the top.

How do you know if you are doing well when you are finally out in the real world?

The real and practical test of whether or not you have done, or are doing, well is when the person who writes your check smiles. Let's look at that in real situations.

How about your senior recital? What constitutes doing well? When you have really pleased your professor and your committee. Whether you feel a piece should be faster or slower, louder or soften, or played with certain mallets is a valid opinion, but a culminating recital is to show your skills as a performer, and your teacher may want you to demonstrate a passage at a softer dynamic level, or show how you can project certain material in the hall, or prove to the committee that you can interpret material in a particular way. So focus totally on performing the music in a way that demonstrates the skills that must be shown to your professor. After the recital is over, you can play the music any way you like. You know you have done well in that major step toward making it to the top if you receive an A.

If you are just starting to get picked up for jobs—perhaps with a touring company or local show band—you can establish your reputation as a good player (or otherwise) very quickly. Dropping a stick during a performance would likely be overlooked, but if you arrive late for a gig, you are not likely to be rehired.

Do what the leader says, even if you feel it would be better done in a different way. Some day, when you are an experienced professional player, the conductor may ask for your opinion or solicit your input in the music. For now, give the conductor/contractor/boss, etc. 110% of what he or she asks—without any attitude.

Summary

If you are serious about making it to the top and becoming the very best, consider these ten steps as the basic ingredients in our recipe. If you don't agree with them, that is even better! They got you thinking, and maybe you are beginning to create your own personalized path to success.

1. Don't play the odds. Someone *will* win that audition and your chances are as good as anyone's.

2. Have an "I can do that" attitude about college jobs. No one will be perfectly qualified for all items in any job description, and you can get to the top by your special strengths.

3. Have a clear and realistic picture of what you are really aiming for and what are your close acceptable options.

4. Create a great resume, or review the one you have in light of the points made earlier.

5. Know how to please the person in charge (conductor, department head, etc.) and how to make him or her look good.

6. Know when to be creative and independent and when to do just as you are told.

7. Work hard to get along with the people you work with and work under. Work especially hard to get along with people who work in support positions under you.

8. Get the best training necessary and the degrees you need, and never stop learning.

9. Be skilled with the latest communications, but never send a mean sounding e-mail.

10. Don't hesitate to laugh at yourself, but be very careful about laughing at others.

When do you know you are at the top?

That answer is simple: when you are happiest in your work. That sounds too simple. But it is so easy to fall into the money trap or be overly focused on promoting yourself. Ask yourself now, as a student, professional, or wherever you are in your career: Are you happy? If you cannot honestly and sincerely answer "yes," you may be in the wrong career. Let's hope that if you answered no, you are early enough in your career that you can make a change and use the "ingredients" in this recipe to guide you. If you answered "yes," then the many who have nurtured you and supported you in your career development can be very proud. ➥

Avoiding Mental Masonry

Christopher Deane

There is a statement that is spoken by virtually all music students at least once, and often many times during their student career. This statement is often heard during moments of frustration when the progress of a given piece of music is slower than expected. This statement can be spoken to provide an alibi for lack of progress in the preparation of a piece. This statement is almost always a prelude to the abandonment of the given piece of music in favor of something deemed more playable by the student. The statement is: "This piece is hard!"

Here is a recipe to help deal with the difficulty of learning a piece of music.

INGREDIENTS:
Positive attitude
Consistent practice
Patience

SERVES:
All musicians at every level.

Upon hearing a student declare that a piece is "hard," I usually adopt an air of faux superiority and ask them, in an all-knowing voice, to repeat their statement. After the usual puzzled look, the student might say, "This piece is hard?" At this moment in the lesson I usually issue the proclamation that the word "hard" will not be allowed from that point on in our lessons—at least in reference to any given piece of music that might be our focus of study.

When asked "Why?" by the student, I will give that student some version of the following observation: *Music isn't hard. A brick wall is hard. Music is time consuming.*

If you look at each piece as being simply a time investment, then any piece can be learned with the proper amount of time allotment. I usually follow this up with the explanation that if one thinks of music as being "hard," then one is building a brick wall between one's initial desire to learn a given piece and the optimism, or constant inspiration, that is required to see such a project through to its successful end.

It might take superhuman ability to break through a hard brick wall. A student might think that the same is true about achieving a breakthrough in learning a "hard" piece of music. Any piece is learnable if one spends the proper amount of time, with healthy patience, to learn it.

Of course, I am aware that any given piece can legitimately be considered difficult. My point is to help the student avoid losing the inspiration for a piece of music due to the technical demands that may exceed the student's abilities at that particular time in his or her studies.

The technical demands that exist in a piece can be the best catalyst for technical growth in the player.

Every piece of music has a gift for the performer. I usually make this statement in close proximity to the "bricks are hard" statement to help the student change how the technical challenge is perceived. I can't remember any piece I have learned, or at least studied, that did not have a "gift" for me either technically or musically. To allow the difficulty of a piece to discourage one from learning it is to refuse the "gift" that the piece of music offers.

For most of us, the initial thoughts of becoming a musician were fueled by the image of music as simply being fun. It can involve an experience of playing music that seemed to come to us easily or music for which we showed a "talent." When a student begins facing the sweat labor that is necessary in becoming a complete musician, it can be discouraging.

Here, then, is the recipe with which to approach a "hard" piece of music.

1. Don't just work to play a passage. Work to be *comfortable* playing the passage.

2. Look at learning a piece of music as an investment of your time. Your frustration comes from the expectation that it should be learned more quickly than is possible for you. Be practical in your process of learning. This means that you should not waste time during the learning process. You must understand that a piece of music takes the time it requires to be learned.

3. Include external forms of discipline in your practicing such as a metronome (to keep you from rushing the process) and an accurate timer to define your entire practice session, as well as the minute-by-minute tasks that good practicing comprises.

4. A good performance comes from making difficult technical issues easier through repetition. This is also true of the mental aspect of performance. Think the same thoughts in the practice room as you do in performance and you will attain consistent results.

5. Seek the "easiest best" way to perform a given passage. There are usually multiple ways to play a passage correctly. Find the easiest way that still gets the job done with quality. ➵

Tasty Charts for the Drumline

Dennis DeLucia

How does a percussion arranger create charts for a marching ensemble in drum corps, band, or "indoor" drumline? He or she must consider the "three I's":

INGREDIENTS:
Implements
Intangibles
Imagination

SERVES:
Marching percussion arrangers.

I.   Implements
   Drums
   Heads
   Sticks
   Accessories

   A.   Instrumentation guide. As a good rule of thumb, the number of percussionists (battery and pit) should account for approximately 20–25% of all musicians in a marching band (e.g., a band of 100 players should include 20–25 percussionists) and 30–35% of all musicians in a drum corps (e.g., 70 brass and 30 percussion).

   B.   Snare drums. Old: 15-inch drums with calfskin or plastic heads; new: 14-inch drums with Kevlar or plastic heads. (I personally do not like 13-inch drums outdoors.)

   C.   Tenors. Old: 15-inch single tenor drums playing simple rhythms that duplicated the snare voice; new: quads or quints ranging in size from 6-inch to 14-inch with plastic heads playing figures that are often *at least* as complex as the snares!

   D.   Bass drums. Old: two identical 10 x 24 drums playing unison quarter notes; new: "tonal" bass drums ranging from 16 to 32 inches with plastic heads and foam muffling playing split figures as fast as thirty-second-note rolls.

   E.   Cymbals. Old: one person playing small (14–16-inch) cymbals with wood handles; new: two to five people playing a variety of cymbals ranging from 17 to 20 inches with leather straps and pads.

   F.   Mallet instruments. Old: none allowed prior to 1974; from 1974–81: "marching" xylophones, bells, and vibes were legal (and unbearably heavy); new: anything goes, with real xylophones, marimbas, vibes, bells, and chimes allowed in the "pit." With the adoption of amplification, these instruments can now be played legitimately, with proper mallets and techniques. And they can be heard!

G.   Pit. Old: none prior to 1982; new: anything goes!

H.   Sticks and mallets. Old: one pair per player, with a penalty for dropping a stick and no replacements allowed; new: carry anything you want, in any quantities.

II. Intangibles
Musical considerations

A.   The Five T's: Time, Technique, Touch, Taste, and Tone (tuning plus stick/mallet plus stroke).

B.   "R.E.S.T.": the best way to play: Relaxed, Efficient, Smooth, Tension-free.

C.   Dynamics: achieved by a uniform degree of wrist-turn from player to player, and not by relying on a ruler, as in 3-inch, 6-inch, 9-inch strokes. Feel, flow, and relaxation are the keys.

D.   Accents: "regular" and "strong" in relation to the dynamic marking.

E.   Individual and ensemble accuracy and expression.

F.   Idiom: the integrity of the musical style or genre.

III. Imagination
The creativity of the writer

Here are 25 rules for writing good arrangements for bands, corps, or "indoor" drumlines:

1.   There are many ways to view the role of percussion in the marching activities. Here are three:

a.   *Percussion drives the car.* It provides the rhythmic drive and momentum for the entire unit. Allow the *battery* to fulfill this role.

b.   *Percussion colors the portrait.* The palette of timbres, textures, and colors that the percussion section can create is infinitely more interesting than brass and woodwinds can provide on a football field or gym floor. Allow the *pit* to lead the way in terms of "color."

c.   *A good drumline is like a good point guard in basketball.* Some are great individual players who don't make their team better, and others are great individual players whose main focus is to make *everyone* around them better! The latter should be the goal of every drumline.

2.   Acknowledge that the arranger must serve two masters:

a.   the integrity of the music at hand;

b.   the *real* talent level (talent capacity) of the players in the ensemble. If the perceived talent level is a 7.2 in terms of difficulty, write a book that is a 7.2 to 7.6. If you write a 9.3 you are serving your own ego rather than serving the real potential for success of your players.

3.   Listen to and research the *original* source of the music.

4. Confer often with the brass/woodwind arranger. Seek his or her input about style, volume, intensity, impact moments, and musical nuance. Work together to create *one* great piece of music, not a percussion chart that does not support and enhance the entire ensemble.

5. Construct a flow chart *before* you write any notes on your manuscript or computer. Use it as a guideline to keep yourself from over-writing. It will help you know where your musical journey (the chart) will *end* before you even *begin*!

6. Know the strengths and limitations of every percussion instrument and accessory.

7. Combine two idioms: the idiom of the original material and the marching music idiom. Don't literally transcribe what's in the original, but make your chart sound and feel good on the big stage that is a football field or gym.

8. Grooves and styles can be identified by the *rhythmic and textural characteristics* of the percussion. For example, a mambo has rhythms that are very different than a samba. And one features a cowbell and the other doesn't!

9. Orchestrate for percussion with the same degree of skill, selectivity, and creativity as Aaron Copland orchestrated for the full orchestra. Create unusual textures: add a triangle to a bells/vibes figure; strike a sizzle cymbal with a 5A in one hand and a felt mallet in the other; play the snare drum with brushes or Hot-Rods or hands.

10. Use plenty of rests and space to allow the music to breathe. Never feel that you must write every instrument into every measure.

11. Write only those figures that will contribute *positively* to the total musical score. If the music doesn't need it, don't write it!

12. Be sure that the *primary* intent of a phrase is crystal clear. If the xylophone is playing the lead line, write sparingly and softly around it so that it will speak clearly. Ditto for any voice or idea.

13. If there is a *secondary* idea, be sure that it is clear and unobtrusive. Anything else is either *color* (a good thing) or *clutter* (bad!).

14. Always keep the *big picture* in mind—the total ensemble statement, the audio/visual impact of the moment.

15. Use instruments and accessories that are appropriate to the composition (e.g., no timbales in "Pines of Rome"!). Research the country/culture origin of instruments and rhythms, and know how and when to use them.

16. Use a variety of *linear* and *vertical (block)* scoring devices to keep your charts fresh and interesting. Don't automatically double the rhythm of the melody with percussion; create interesting counter-rhythmic lines and accents.

17. Avoid writing rhythms that conflict. Sixteenth notes against triplets might work with trumpet and clarinet (legato), but would sound cluttered and distorted on snare and quints (too staccato).

18. Write plenty of dynamics, accents, and expression markings on the chart. Don't expect any teacher or player to interpret exactly what you had in mind.

19. Tune and stage the ensemble properly *for the music at hand*. "Groove" music has different requirements than "classical" or "straight-ahead" music does. Account for the differences.

20. Avoid the temptation to keep the mallet players needlessly busy by writing annoying, unmusical chordal rolls that (badly) duplicate a chord that already exists in the brass/woodwind ensemble. Remember: if the music doesn't need it, don't write it!

21. Do not double the keyboards with the woodwinds very often. This *can* be an interesting device if used sparingly and wisely, but it can create or exacerbate pitch and/or rhythm problems. Be creative: sometimes think of the mallet choir as one gigantic piano.

22. Consider that the success of any written music is dependent upon a combination of the writer, the teachers (staff), and the performers. As the arranger, you control the art of the chart, but you must accept responsibility for the potential of the performers to achieve their goal.

23. Ask yourself if the brass/woodwind ensemble sounds better or worse once the percussion is added.

24. Be willing to re-write and improve the chart after you've heard the full ensemble and seen the drill.

25. Re-write it again...and again...and again!

The finished product is your personal work of art and, like cooking a great meal, it takes time to create, to prepare, and to enjoy. So, *enjoy!* ➼

RECIPE

Savoring the Sounds

Robin Engelman

The complex, unpredictable overtones of resonant percussion instruments—gongs, tam-tams, and cymbals—are rendered inaudible when combined with diatonically tuned instruments. Thus, they are best served unaccompanied.

INGREDIENTS:
1 quiet room
1 gong, tam-tam or large suspended cymbal
1 comfortable stool
2 beaters

SERVES:
Musicians

Gently strike the instrument with beaters.

Allow the sound to disappear before re-striking.

Experiment with places to strike and ways of striking.

Never hurry.

Listen, always.

Ride Cymbal a la Mode

Peter Erskine

This tasty *bon mot* will help a drummer develop the sweetest cymbal sound possible. The fantastic thing about this recipe is that it can serve anywhere from one to one hundred! Characteristics of this dish include both touch and rhythmic feel. (Note: proper preparation of *Ride Cymbal a la Mode* does not require as much stirring as a well-played brush beat!)

INGREDIENTS:
1 ride cymbal, 18" to 22" inches in diameter
1 cymbal stand (flush-base model preferred)
1 drumstick (suitable for ride cymbal playing, i.e., not too heavy and with not-too-large a tip)
1 drum throne
1 metronome
1 drummer

SERVES:
The music! This also serves the drummer, the rest of the rhythm section, and the entire band as well as the conductor—not to mention the listeners.

Directions
1. First, prepare the ingredients as follows:

   a. Set up the ride cymbal on the cymbal stand so that you can comfortably play the cymbal.

   b. Seat height should equal how you normally sit at the drumset.

   c. I recommend that the cymbal not be placed any higher than your shoulder. The cymbal should also be relatively flat, i.e., not tilted at an extreme angle; it will sound better this way, and will enable you to make optimum contact on the cymbal with your stick.

   d. Preheat your metronome to a tempo that equals 60 beats per minute; this will be the quarter-note pulse for starters. Do not turn on the metronome's sound at this time, however.

2. Next, begin exploring the tone of the cymbal. Assuming that you have been able to select a good cymbal from the market, each individual stroke on the cymbal should produce a sound that is pleasing to you. While drummers often engage in the quest for *speed*, our first concern here is entirely on *sound*.

(A trumpet player recently asked me how I warm up and practice; I replied that I played long tones. His initial reaction was to laugh, but then he "got" what I was talking about: Tone is one of the most important things for musicians to achieve on their instrument, though it is often one of the more overlooked aspects of drumming.)

So, start off by playing single notes on the cymbal—long tones, i.e., whole notes.

   a.   The mechanics involved in producing a good tone on the cymbal include using gravity as well as the weight of your arm when bringing the stick down to play on the cymbal. While some drummers advocate a relatively high rebound after each stroke, I recommend that you work on building a consistent and relaxed rebound of only 1–2 inches in height.

   b.   My technique includes the use of my right hand's middle finger as the fulcrum or balance point, with the thumb positioned on top of the stick as it strikes the cymbal. The stroke is a combination of arm, wrist, and finger movement, all of which should contribute to draw the sound out of the cymbal.

3.   Turning on the metronome, play a series of whole notes, half notes, and then quarter notes in sync with the metronome's pulse.

   a.   I find it helpful to think of (or sing) the triplet subdivisions of the jazz syncopation while playing quarter notes on the ride. This, in effect, carves out the proper space between the notes and will train your body and ears to play in the most accurate and style-faithful manner possible.

   b.   Gradually increase the speed of the metronome.

   c.   You might want to turn the metronome off while playing, continuing the quarter-note pulse on the ride for eight or sixteen measures, and then turn the metronome back on while still playing. How steady is your time? Keeping a practice diary or log is helpful in noting your tempo strengths and weaknesses.

4.   Now let's add the syncopated ride pattern. Set the metronome to a temperature of 88.

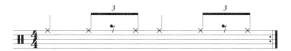

   a.   The basic arm motion should not change when you add the syncopated/triplet rhythm on the "&" of beats 2 and 4. Each note should lead to the next quarter note (just like the bass player's "walking" quarter-note pulse). Ultimately, the phrasing of the jazz ride cymbal pattern is each drummer's signature, and so any variations in the use of accent spices is up to you!

   b.   The phrasing of the syncopated ride rhythm will change as the tempo increases. Fast tempos will yield a straighter eighth-note feel than a slow tempo. The best way to hear, learn, and find your own cymbal beat phrasing is to listen to as many jazz drummer recordings and performances as possible.

Preparations for Serving

1. Practice!

2. Play along with jazz recordings, such as those made by Miles Davis during the late 1950s/ early 1960s; the Count Basie Big Band, plus bebop recordings by Art Blakey, Max Roach, the Cannonball Adderley bands, Buddy Rich, *et al.* As I tell my students: If you can make the music feel good with just one hand, then you know you're onto something.

Presentation

1. Add the hi-hat playing on beats 2 and 4 with the left foot. I submit that it is always a good idea to start simple when playing with a band; this will always give the drummer and the music room to grow. When adding rhythms with the left hand or bass drum, the ride cymbal pattern, as well as intensity and feel, should not inadvertently change! Consistency is all-important when dishing out *Ride Cymbal a la Mode*.

2. In addition to consistency, strive to find a proper dynamic level of volume with which to best blend with the other ingredients in the music.

3. Make it swing!

4. For added calories, add a fat backbeat when appropriate.

Clean Up

Served properly, there should little or no mess for you to worry about. The drummer who can swing, however, will "clean up" when it comes to getting the best jazz gigs in town! ➵

Vocabulary Crock Pot Stew

Neal Flum

This recipe provides educational nutrition in the form of "vocabularies" for battery drummers and drumset players seeking to become fundamentally sound with their skill-set and more expressive through their musicianship.

INGREDIENTS:
A cup of rhythm reading vocabulary
A cup of rudiment vocabulary
A cup of *Stick Control* vocabulary
A cup of dynamics and articulations
A generous dash of self-discipline
A generous dash of desire
A healthy dash of work ethic

SERVES:
Any percussionist, regardless of skill-set level.

Directions
Combine all ingredients in a consistent and diligent practice routine.

Engage a dedicated and enthusiastic teacher to help keep watch over the crock pot.

Add as much inspiration as the crock pot will hold.

Simmer for as long as you desire to improve yourself as a musician. Learning is a life-long process.

I love words. They are fascinating vessels of thought capable of doing so much. Their utility as tools of communication is immeasurable. Without them the world would be a vastly different and, dare I say, emptier place. Being able to share our affection with a loved one; comfort a friend in difficult times; make a colleague laugh; teach a student a skill—all are made possible by words. In a very important sense, they also make us who we are and they provide for us the ability to think as well as offer us a mode for conveying our ideas and feelings.

The many words that populate our relationships, our vocations, all that we do, find as their home vocabularies. You might hear the terms lexicon, terminology, vernacular, *et al.* But when we come right down to it, they are all in some sense vocabularies. Having access to and developing those vocabularies provides for us the possibility of being more expressive in our interactions with others and making our lives more meaningful.

In much same the way, as percussionists, we can learn vocabularies that will not only make it possible for us to be more expressive as musicians, but will also help us to develop the soundest of foundations for our skill-set and its continued development. The goal of this essay is to share with you three vocabularies that will help you develop a skill-set at the most fundamental level and beyond, and also assist you in becoming more expressive as a musician. In whatever we do, enriching our vocabularies will allow us to more successfully engage the world in which we live and, perhaps, using the power of words, change that world as well.

As percussionists we have words. Our words for the purpose of this essay can be rhythms, rudiments, and combinations of single beats, double beats, and triple beats that we will now define as *Stick Control* groupings. Our words can function on both a fundamental level (our skill-set) and a secondary level (expression through application—music). The more words we have at our disposal, the more fundamentally sound and expressive we can be and the more capable we can become as performers.

Of course, the words we have available to us and the words we actually use have as their proper home a *vocabulary*. Placing our words, the language of percussion, into different vocabularies allows us a more organized process for seeking them out and, hopefully, mastering them. Knowing where anything is always makes it easier to find it. As my Mom liked to say, "A place for everything and everything in its place."

Beyond the basic skills we learn and develop as percussionists is the need to communicate. That is how we *make music*. That is how we share one of our most basic needs as human beings: expressing ourselves. We can be far more expressive, of course, if we have a greater vocabulary for doing so, be it as musicians or in interacting with others in the various aspects of our lives.

Having and developing performance skills and seeking to employ those skills in expressing ourselves musically as percussionists can be enhanced by three particular vocabularies: a rhythm reading vocabulary, a rudiments vocabulary, and a *Stick Control* vocabulary. These are the building-block vocabularies of becoming a more fundamentally sound and more musical percussionist.

Please remember that there are always more words to learn and other languages as well. And as our musical language becomes more nuanced through the use of dynamics, articulations, timbres, etc., our vocabulary offers us the opportunity for more sophisticated levels of expression.

Reading

Reading helps us build our rhythm vocabulary. Reading and understanding rhythms allows us to engage its practical application, music. And reading more music allows us to function better as performers, as individuals, and in ensembles as well. Sight-reading is invaluable for any musician. Think about a studio musician unable to sight-read well. You get the picture.

Simply put, we should read as much as possible. It's no secret that students who read more tend to write better and thus communicate better. In developing our rhythm vocabulary, we might seek out Thom Hannum's *Championship Concepts for Marching Percussion* workbook and check out his material on "The Check Patterns and Duple and Triplet Variations." The "check patterns" and variations will be a helpful resource for engaging the fundamental rhythm reading vocabulary we all need as percussionists. The "check patterns" and variations provide not only a vocabulary but a systematic process for aiding our reading and sight-reading and allowing us to teach ourselves as well. The "check patterns" and variations approach to reading also includes the physical element of assigning natural *stickings* to our rhythms. Combining different learning channels for engaging reading makes the process far more accessible and achievable for us as percussionists.

Rudiments

To increase our ability to express ourselves and read as well, we should also learn our rudiments. Rudiments are another vocabulary that we can combine with the "check patterns" and variations for developing our skill-set and expressiveness. PAS offers a list of rudiments on its Website (www.pas.org), and there are many other sources as well.

Rudiments offer us the possibility of being more skilled and meaningful as percussionists. They are what we might term *essential* vocabulary words—the drumming primer, if you will.

Rudiments also connect us with all those percussionists who have come before us. Rudiments have great historical significance and have enjoyed a high level of usefulness throughout their history. Isn't it neat that we can play the same rudiments that were played long ago by other percussionists? Isn't it also neat that some of these rudiments take on a slightly different expression, much like words, as they are used in this particular time with somewhat different mindsets and different instruments and implements? Playing rudiments is like reading a great book from ages ago; it connects us to the past and allows us to understand the past in our current mindset.

Beyond the connectivity we enjoy with percussionists of the past, rudiments provide an essential playing foundation. Whether it be marching percussion or playing drumset, rudiments play a vital role in what we do.

Stick Control

Also important as a vocabulary for the developing and advancing percussionist is George Stone's book *Stick Control*. This text offers any percussionist both a method and a vocabulary for engaging the basic elements of percussion: single beats, double beats, and triple beats in their many groupings and variations of those groupings. It is a resource that has been available since 1936, and its utility as an aid in building fundamental skills is no less important today than it was back then.

Practicing the *Stick Control* patterns is a lot like drilling the spelling of words or working sentences to learn the basics of grammar. To add another level of expression to the *Stick Control* vocabulary, we can study out of Stone's text *Accents and Rebounds*. Like *Stick Control*, it is an invaluable source of words for our growing vocabulary as percussionists.

A well-read percussionist who has engaged the vocabularies shared above and who continues to enrich those vocabularies and add other vocabularies as well will, with attention to skill-set development, become a sounder and more expressive musician. As I write this piece, I look at my bookcase and see many texts that are available for vocabulary building: Ted Reed's *Syncopation*, Jim Chapin's *Advanced Techniques for the Modern Drummer*, Ed Uribe's *The Essence of Afro-Cuban Percussion*, and the list goes on. As percussionists, we have to be multi-lingual—and that's a good thing.

Writing this essay would not have been possible without words. I hope that the words I have chosen will inspire you to develop your own vocabularies for engaging the rewarding art of percussion. The three vocabularies I have offered you, like a wonderful meal, should always prove satisfying and leave you wanting to enjoy that experience time and time again as you build and advance your skill-set and, at the same time, become more expressive in all you do, musically speaking.

Thankfully, there are no calories in the vocabularies we can learn about and engage, but rather an endless possibility of our words combined in the grammar of music yielding great satisfaction for us as performers. Within each of us is the desire to express ourselves. How much more fundamentally sound our skill-set will be and how much richer our ability to express ourselves musically will be with plentiful vocabularies and the desire to cherish and increase those vocabularies with more words. Maybe you will be a musician who, with your words, changes the world.

Dedicated to my mother, Roslyn J. Flum, for her words of support and encouragement. ➤●

Finding Musical Expression in Marimba Performance

Mark Ford

How does a musical performance go from an academic reading of the manuscript to an expressive emotional connection with an audience? Developing your expressive interpretation of the music you play is one of the most important and satisfying aspects of music making. Your interpretation reflects your ideas and feelings about the music.

Unfortunately, younger musicians usually concentrate only on understanding the notes and rhythms of a marimba solo. Obviously this is important, but it's only fifty percent of the job. Communicating your emotional connection with the music through your interpretation is essential to the "magic" of music. Think about how a certain performance or piece of music has touched you in the past. When you perform, you want to connect with an audience in the same manner.

The following ideas may be helpful as you prepare a piece of music and try to get "beyond the notes and rhythms" to find a starting point for your interpretation. Remember, the goal when playing music is to be expressive while maintaining stylistic considerations.

INGREDIENTS:
A marimba and mallets
A marimba solo
A regular practice routine
Your imagination

Optional spices:
A music library
Marimba recordings
Casals and the Art of Interpretation by David Blum (Holmes and Meier Publishers, 1977)

SERVES:
Marimbists at all levels.

Directions

Understand the Style of Music
Once you select a marimba solo to perform, it is important to understand the stylistic considerations of the music. If you are preparing a transcription of a Prelude by J.S. Bach and you are unfamiliar with music of the Baroque period, then your interpretation may not be convincing. It would be impossible to perform a transcription well without studying and

listening to the original version. Whether your selection is an original composition or a transcription, the understanding of the music and composer's intentions are vital to the success of your performance. Here are some starting points:

- Study the score carefully and learn as much as you can about the composer.

- Listen to recordings of the composer's music and determine which stylistic considerations and expressive elements are important in your solo.

- Be aware of these expressive elements when you listen to other instrumentalists perform.

- Define unfamiliar musical terms on the manuscript.

Identify the Phrase Structure

The integrity of musical phases, or the grouping of notes, is essential to your interpretation. Listen to how a violinist or French horn player begins and ends a phrase. Slurring is an important tool musicians use to connect notes and develop phrases. Wind/string players and vocalists can easily glide from one note to the next without re-articulating the subsequent notes. Unfortunately, keyboard percussion instruments do not have this capability.

Slurs can be imitated on the marimba by re-attacking the second note at a softer dynamic to blend into the ring of the first note. Even though at best marimbists can only imitate a slur, it is important to listen carefully to how other instrumentalists utilize the slur. By understanding how a wind player or violinist shapes a phrase with slurring, the marimbist can be more sensitive to the development of phrases on the marimba. Critical listening is necessary for a strong interpretation.

As you learn the notes and stickings for the music, mark the beginnings and endings of each musical phrase in pencil on the manuscript. Strive to make the delivery of each phrase crystal clear to the listener. Just playing the right notes and the right rhythms will not be enough to make your playing expressive.

1. A phrase should have musical direction and an ending.

2. Decide on the musical "character" of the phrase. Is it moving forward (building), pulling away (relaxing), or unchanging?

3. Practice singing the phrase the way you want to play it.

4. Ask yourself, "Is my interpretation of the phrase interesting to me?" If your answer is "no" or "I'm not sure," then it probably won't be interesting to the audience.

5. Record your playing regularly.

6. Use a pencil to mark areas in the music that need attention as you listen to your recording.

Dynamic Inflection

Most performers strive to utilize the composer's dynamic intentions as written on the music. However, there are many "shades" or levels to each of the standard dynamic markings. Rarely does a piece of music keep a static dynamic level, even though it looks that way on the page. Most solos have an ebb and flow of relative dynamics under a heading such as *forte* or *piano*. It is up to the performer to decide how to incorporate this dynamic motion into an interpretation of each phrase.

1. Focus on the page of music and utilize all of the information the composer has given you regarding dynamics.

2. Analyze the shape of the phrase and the musical direction of each phrase. If the composer does not offer any suggestions, try a basic application of higher pitches equal louder dynamics (fuller dynamics at phrase peaks). Decide if this fits the direction and style of the music.

3. Try different approaches to sample different dynamic applications.

4. Once you have become satisfied with your ideas, write them in pencil on the music.

5. Record your interpretation and make revisions if necessary.

Thinking About Time

Percussionists have a tendency to think that rhythm and time are rigid, like a grid. Just take out your metronome and set it to sub-divide sixteenth notes to listen to this grid. Non-percussionists, such as pianists and violinists, do not always think in this manner. Listen to other instrumentalists and focus on how they use time and rhythm to be expressive. Study the music of these performances as you listen to "rubato" and "expressivo" sections of the music. You will find that there are many possible variations of the same rhythm.

1. Analyze your music for opportunities to utilize time (pushing forward, pulling back, *accel*, *ritard*, etc.). Cadential points are prime targets.

2. Always consider the style of music when deciding the appropriate ways to use time in your playing. Remember, too much of a good thing can cause the listener to "tune out."

3. Consider consistent roll speed with dynamic variation for help in musical phrase direction.

Articulation Possibilities

Even though the marimba may seem to have limited articulation possibilities, there are many ways to alter the tone and attack of the marimba for expressive content. Changing stroke types (such as legato and staccato strokes) and using different mallets are common choices for articulation shifts on the marimba. Choosing and combining different mallets can offer articulation changes for the listener. Combining the top part of the marimba mallet in one hand versus the normal playing area in the other hand (and other possibilities such as striking with the shaft of the marimba mallets) are other options. Some composers utilize dry stokes or dead strokes for shorter articulations, where the mallet strikes the bar and remains on the bar to dampen the sound. Different playing areas on the marimba bars (near the nodes, halfway to the center of the bar, and the center of the bar) also create a simulation of articulation shifts.

1. Try different articulations as a means for expressive playing, not just an effect. Do not rely solely on mallet choice, but listen to the marimba and experiment with different stroke types.

2. Since most composers do not mark these articulation shifts, identify the sections of the music you think are applicable and experiment with different playing areas on the bars, mallets, etc.

3. Test your articulation shifts in a large room or performance hall. These changes will sound different in a big room as compared to the practice room.

4. Record your performance and mark any necessary adjustments on your music.

Recommended Reading and Listening

An excellent text on musical interpretation is *Casals and the Art of Interpretation* by David Blum. Based on the teachings of cellist/orchestral director Pablo Casals, this short text is a classic work on interpretation and expression. Casals states, "The simplest things in music are the ones that count. The simplest things are, of course, also the most difficult to achieve and take years of work." Students of all ages will benefit from Casals' ideas as they are demonstrated through a variety of orchestral examples. The concepts are clear even if the reader is unfamiliar with the multitude of musical examples. However, listening to the examples and score study will lead to a broader understanding of musical interpretation.

Additionally, it is important to vary your listening habits with many styles of music. Attend concerts by professional musicians as often as possible. Put yourself in the position to hear "unfamiliar" music played by outstanding musicians, whether in concert or on recordings. This could include any solo recital, chamber music, jazz, world music, and orchestra concerts. Over time, these experiences with quality music, combined with a sensitive approach to phrasing, will give you the foundation for expressive performances. ♪

Snare Drum Gumbo

Guy G. Gauthreaux II

Preparing a snare drum solo for a recital, contest, or audition requires slow, steady baking. Think of your practice room as a warm oven in which you are going to let the piece slowly cook—not a microwave in which you can zap your solo in a matter of minutes.

INGREDIENTS:

Snare drum solo one to three minutes in length (do not substitute a page from an exercise book)
1 pair snare drum sticks
1 snare drum, recently tuned
1 snare drum stand, height and tilt adjustable
1 snare drum mute, to taste
A working knowledge of snare drum rudiments, appropriate to age
1 audio recording of solo, full-length version
1 to 2 music stands, as needed
1 pencil
1 metronome
1 practice pad
1 mirror
1 mini disk recorder

SERVES:

Anyone preparing a snare drum solo for a recital, contest, or audition.

Preparation

If required for a contest, be sure to select a solo from the locally prescribed list. If you are not sure, check with a local band or orchestra director. Sometimes, music stores have copies of the local required solo lists and often stock all solos on these lists. Most snare drum solos by Warren Benson, Art Cappio, Michael Colgrass, Jacques Delecluse, David P. Eyler, Guy Gauthreaux, Marty Hurley, Mitch Markovich, John S. Pratt, Garwood Whaley, Charles Wilcoxon, John Wooton, etc. will work in most situations. My personal favorites include my "American Suite" and "Recital Piece," Benson's "Three Dances," Colgrass's "Six Unaccompanied Solos," and Markovitch's "Tornado." Traditional rudimental solos like "The Downfall of Paris" and "Three Camps" can work well for young students. Keep the solo length to about one to three minutes. Anything longer is just too much snare drum music for any person to digest!

Choose a pair of matched sticks that fits your hands and is suitable for the drum you are using. If you tap the shoulder of each stick on your head (lightly!) the pitch of each stick should be the same or very nearly the same. Marching sticks on a concert snare drum should always be avoided as the results will be terrible. For concert playing on most snare drums, I prefer to use the Cooperman #7 (the rosewood model for heavy work and the persimmon model for lighter playing). Concert sticks by Reamer and Innovative Percussion also work well in most situations. For the budget minded (especially younger players), the Vic Firth SD1 is a good choice.

You can use most any snare drum for this recipe, as long as it has new or nearly new heads (top and bottom), has all the snares, and is perfectly round. Every snare drum should be tuned by someone who knows how to tune a drum and has actual first-hand knowledge of what a good snare drum should sound like. If a snare drum is tuned properly, it will sound good with almost any player. If it is not tuned properly, it will sound bad with any player.

Spending big bucks on a drum does not ensure a great sound for the life of the drum. You have to maintain the tuning, especially after the purchase. I keep the top and bottom heads of most of my snare drums tuned to an A or A-flat. My personal snare drum of choice is a 7-inch Lang-Gladstone black lacquer wood shell, with semi-custom Freer snares, a medium Aquarian Modern Vintage batter head, a Remo Ambassador or Diplomat clear snare head, and some slight tension on the built-in felt muffle system. This drum works great for almost all snare drum solos. I also like to use my Black Swamp (5.5-inch brass Multisonic) when performing outdoors, or when I just want a brighter sound that will cut through in most performance or recording situations.

The height of the snare drum should be high enough to accommodate the player without leaning over, and low enough to avoid accidental rimshots. Place the top head near the player's waist line and you will be close to the perfect height. The drum can be tilted down and to the right for traditional-grip players, or perfectly level for matched-grip players. Although some younger players tilt the drum down to the front, or down towards the player, these drum positions can negatively affect how the sound of the drum will travel.

To avoid page turns, any solo printed in excess of three pages will require two music stands (or one music stand along with a plastic music stand extender; e.g., "Stand Out").

Cooking

When possible, listen to a recording of the solo. For many standard contest solos (and rudiments), recordings can be found on the CDs *Open-Close-Open* and *Rudiments! Rudiments! Rudiments!* Seven older traditional snare drum solos and the original 26 rudiments can also be found on Frank Arsenault's *Twenty Six Standard Rudiments*. Some Websites also have excellent recordings and videos of snare drum rudiments (e.g., vicfirth.com).

When you begin preparing the solo, be sure you understand all rhythms, grace notes, time signatures, and special effects. If necessary, contact a local drum teacher for guidance. Once you are sure of these items, start to work out the music, measure by measure if necessary, and then line by line. During this stage, I cannot stress enough the importance of working at a moderately slow tempo. Many students (and professionals alike) like to practice at fast tempos, often times learning passages incorrectly.

Once you can play all rhythms and grace notes, begin to put complete sections together. To keep your interest peaked during these workout sessions, always begin and end your practice with a section of the solo you can already play correctly. Never walk away from the drum when you are having difficulties. Work things out to a point where you can play them correctly (or play through an easier section), and then take a break.

As a general rule, try not to memorize a solo until you can play it through completely and correctly. Once memorized, go back and read through the music at least once a week to be sure you have not forgotten any details (dynamics, tempo changes, etc.).

Try to have the snare drum solo prepared to play in its entirety (without stopping) one month before the contest, audition, or recital. During the month prior to the first performance, refocus on dynamics, tempo, and phrasing. During the last week, play the solo completely through with no stops at least once a day. After each daily run-through, correct, polish, and repair any sections that still need attention.

In case of last-minute unforeseen technical problems with flams, drags, diddles, etc., be prepared to simplify these rudiments. This is a last-resort fix and it will ultimately affect your overall grade, ratings, or audition ranking.

On all copies of music to be used by a judge or audition committee, lightly number each printed measure of the music with a pencil. As a general rule, avoid re-numbering measures in repeated strains. ━●

Successful Time Playing in a Jazz Combo

Danny Gottlieb

In my role as a full-time Assistant Professor of Jazz Studies at the University of North Florida, one of my goals is to help drum students develop the skills needed to perform with a jazz group on a professional level. *The* most essential requirement is to play good basic jazz time in an appropriate style with a good feel, touch, sound, dynamics, and sensitivity. Before moving on to advanced time concepts, I try to make sure that all the basic elements of jazz drumming have been discussed, analyzed, and perfected.

INGREDIENTS:
Drumsticks
Drumset
CD player or iPod
Metronome
CDs or MP3 downloads of jazz drummers playing standard jazz songs
Lead sheets with the melody and form of the songs (from *The Real Book*, etc.)
Notepad and pen or pencil
Video or audio recorder, if possible

SERVES:
Any drummer, on any level, wishing to improve his or her performance in a jazz combo.

Preparing the Meal
First we must describe the specific meal that we are making, as with jazz drumming there are many variations. We are talking about preparing a drummer for performance in a jazz combo. What exactly are the elements that make up a successful jazz combo drummer?

I. **Understanding what a jazz drummer does in a combo.**

    A. Plays time
    B. Accompanies the group in playing the melody of the song
    C. Accompanies the soloist
    D. Plays a drum solo or trades phrases with the soloist

II. **Types of rhythms needed**

    A. Swing feel rhythms

        1. Two-beat
        2. Four-beat
        3. Backbeat, cross-stick, and rim
        4. Shuffle

     5. Hi-hat on 2 and 4
     6. Broken hi-hat
     7. Comping variations

  B. Straight eighth-note rhythms

     1. Bossa nova
     2. Samba
     3. Latin
     4. Broken straight-eighth
     5. Rock
     6. Funk

Let's make a meal from these ingredients with practice exercises.

Swing Feels for a Jazz Combo
Listen to some jazz drummer recordings to see how jazz beats sound when played by the jazz greats. Possible jazz drummers include Joe Morello, Max Roach, Buddy Rich, Mel Lewis, Jimmy Cobb, Philly Joe Jones, Art Blakey, Roy Haynes, Elvin Jones, Tony Williams, Kenny Clarke, Shelly Manne, Harold Jones, and Louie Bellson.

Take your notepad and a pen or pencil. When you listen to the recordings, analyze the following and write down any specifics for the following questions:

I. What is the drummer playing on the cymbal?

    A. The beat
    B. The volume
    C. The actual notes
    D. Is it consistent, or does it change?

II. What type of comping rhythm is the drummer playing on the snare? (Comping is the term used to describe the snare accents played by a jazz drummer. It comes from the word accompany or accompaniment.)

    A. Single notes.
    B. Multiple notes.
    C. Patterns or rhythms combined with the bass drum.
    D. Patterns or rhythms combined with the hi-hat and bass drum.
    E. How does the snare comping relate to the song or the soloist?
    F. Are there dynamics (rises and falls) in the snare part?

III. What is the drummer playing on the bass drum?

    A. 4/4.
    B. 1 and 3.
    C. Broken comping.
    D. Independent rhythms from the ride cymbal.
    E. Rhythms with the ride cymbal.

IV. How does the comping relate to the melody of the song? As the selection analyzed is a standard song, it should be easy to obtain a copy of the melody. Look at the rhythms and melody of the song. Sing along with the song, and note where the drummer plays fills and comping rhythms.

A. Does the drummer play rhythms that *are* the melody of the song?
B. Does the drummer play *around* the melody of the song?
C. Does the drummer fill in around the melody?

Now that we have fully analyzed what the drummer has played, let's move to the drumset.

I. Copy the cymbal rhythm from the recording.

A. Try to memorize the sound of the cymbal rhythm from the recording.
B. Using the metronome, note the tempo of the song. Our goal is to play the cymbal rhythm at that speed.
C. If it is a tempo that is easy to play, try to duplicate the cymbal rhythm with the recording. If it is a fast tempo, slow the metronome down and play the cymbal rhythm at a manageable, slower tempo, until you feel comfortable, and then slowly speed up the metronome. Continue practicing until you reach the desired tempo.

II. Add the bass drum and hi-hat.

A. At first, try playing the hi-hat on 2 and 4, and the bass drum lightly on all four beats, and on 1 and 3. This may not be exactly what the drummer is playing on the recording, but it will center the beat and help you gain a balance on the drumset. After you feel comfortable with this four-limb feel, it's time to copy the actual comping approach.
B. Play along with the recording many, many times. Each time through, try to copy more and more of the feel, sound, and actual notes of the original drummer. This will help develop an authentic jazz feel.

III. Record your sound and feel.

A. Record yourself playing the actual feel.
B. Record yourself playing along with the recording.
C. Listen back and analyze.

    1. Does it sound the way you thought it did while playing?
    2. Are you satisfied with the sound?
    3. What can be improved?
    4. Does it sound authentic?
    5. Ask qualified musicians to listen to the recording. They may offer helpful suggestions.

IV. Create your own variations. Now that you have experience with an authentic jazz feel, you can devise variations for practice and musical development.

A. Try different types of comping. Play along with the song, but make up your own rhythms.
B. Devise practice exercises based on the rhythms played by the drummer on the recording. Take one phrase, or idea, and find variations.

    1. Play a snare part on the bass drum or a bass part on the snare.
    2. Vary the cymbal rhythm.
    3. Play some rhythms on the bass drum and cymbal together, or on the snare and cymbal together.
    4. Play the entire song with the left hand or bass drum while keeping the ride cymbal pattern constant.

5. Try the Adam Nussbaum exercise: Play triplets, hand to hand, accenting the melody within the triplets. You can play this with the bass drum on all four beats, and the hi-hat on 2 and 4, or with other foot combinations.

6. Put the metronome on 1 and 3 or on 2 and 4 while practicing.

7. Try faster and slower tempos.

8. Try different dynamics.

V. Apply this approach for the other swing feels.

    A. 2-beat and 4-beat. In the recordings analyzed, note whether the bass player is playing half notes (1 and 3), or walking bass (all four beats). The drummer will adjust the time feel based on the time feel generated by the bass player, and both approaches are very different and specific. Also, If the cymbal rhythm is played by the drummer on the hi-hat, proper attention must be given to developing the same great swing feel on the hi-hat.

    B. Backbeat, cross-stick, and rim. In some instances, especially when the combo is accompanying a singer, the drummer with play the swing feel with a 2 and 4 backbeat, or a cross-stick backbeat. Analyze, note, and copy.

    C. Shuffle. A classic swing rhythm with many variations. Here are drummer suggestions for shuffle: Mel Lewis, Buddy Rich, Bernard Purdie, Jeff Porcaro, Steve Jordan, Steve Gadd.

    D. Hi-hat on 2 and 4, and broken hi-hat comping variations. The standard jazz patterns usually have the hi-hat on 2 and 4. However, many modern jazz innovators have placed the hi-hat, for orchestration, feel, and comping purposes, in different part of the measure, and in different parts of the patterns. Most of the time, these hi-hat variations are spontaneous improvisation. Master drummers for analysis include Tony Williams, Elvin Jones, and Jack DeJohnette.

VI. Repeat the same process for bossa nova, Latin, samba, broken straight-eighth, rock, and funk.

    A. Bossa nova.

        1. Drummer suggestions: Stan Getz bossa nova recordings from the 1960s; any bossa nova recording.

        2. Songs might include: "Girl from Ipenema," "Wave," "Triste"

        3. Make sure the bass drum, hi-hat and snare patterns are correct and have the proper feel.

    B. Latin.

        1. There are many books on Latin rhythms applied to the drumset. For combo drumming, I suggest a combination of reviewing these rhythmic patterns and then the listening/copy process as described above. Pancho Sanchez is one suggestion for listening and analysis.

        2. Many recordings feature a variety of Latin percussion instruments, such as timbales, bongos, and conga parts. For drumset, the idea is to copy the rhythmic patterns with drumset elements (hi-hat, cowbell, toms, snare, bass drum) in a way that reflects authenticity and groove.

C. Samba

    1. Samba recordings must be analyzed using the same method.

    2. Jazz combo samba suggested drummers: Airto (Chick Corea, own recordings); Mark Walker (Caribbean Jazz Project, own recordings); Mike Shapiro

D. Broken Straight-Eighth feel

    1. This is the famous "ECM" recording feel. Eighth-note patterns are played with variations, as with swing jazz.

    2. Drummer suggestions: Jack DeJohnette, Bob Moses, myself.

E. Rock and funk.

    1. There are rock and funk elements in the jazz combo. There are many recordings for analysis.

    2. Drummers include: Peter Erskine, Rod Morgenstein, Dave Weckl, Vinnie Colaiuta, Bernard Purdie, Dave Garibaldi, Steve Smith.

Now, eat the meal and enjoy! After extensive analysis, preparation, practice, and understanding, you are ready to perform the basic beats and feels required of the combo jazz drummer! ➡●

It's Time

Gordon Gottlieb

As "time" is perhaps the single most essential ingredient in a drummer/percussionist's stew, a musician should be able to establish a healthy working relationship with a click track or metronome. I've found that many musicians have developed and accept a passive time sense (outer-directed, conducted, or metronome-led) in preference to an active time sense (from within; inner pulse). With so many physical, emotional, and technical variables within every musician, it becomes a necessity to forge a healthy and continuing relationship with a metronome for stability and grounding—and inner pulse.

INGREDIENTS:
Heartbeat
Metronome
Any available rhythm-producing agent

SERVES:
Inner pulse
Humanity

Since the timekeeping role is usually assumed by the drummer/percussionist/timpanist in live situations, a sure time sense is of great value. However, great flexibility must be cultivated as well. This is particularly applicable to orchestral percussionists who are often in the position of anticipating whether or not the brass section will drag, the strings will rush, etc., and who very often are obliged to synchronize their time sense to those without one—including the conductor!

All political analogies aside, usually the strongest instrumental voice(s) will dictate the group approach to a rhythmic motive or phrase in a live context, serving as an internal conductor. My teacher, Saul Goodman, always reminded me of the timpanist's role: to *lead* the orchestra. Of course, this necessitates possession of a firm sense of time, incorporating awareness of tempo deviations and/or departures, as well as a good tempo memory—for instance, at various section points in a composition (in studio parlance, "perfect click").

In terms of the studio, Mel Lewis told me that in the early days of recording there was no click track, and all tempo responsibilities were left to the drummer. So if a take ran shorter or longer than the prescribed length of a composition, Mel would have to count off a suitably slower or faster tempo so that the length was exactly 60 seconds, or whatever. This was a very precarious method, to be sure, but evidently drummers were able to gauge their time senses accordingly.

Of course, the click track has eliminated concerns of timing, but has posed different challenges, most importantly, that of exact synchronization.

Since music is a humanly based art form, it would seem at first somewhat Faustian and truly diabolical to have to make music with an unforgiving, relentless machine ticking in your headphones like a clock in a nightmare. However, if you can imagine the click as an instrument such as claves or a woodblock, you should be able to achieve a more organic rapport. As guitarist Steve Khan has remarked, "The click is your friend." Developing this friendship should be an interesting and fun process, with a confident inner pulse as your objective.

Since percussion playing necessitates varying degrees of distance and attack with mallets, sticks, or hands and fingers on a spectrum of instruments, creative practice methods are an inevitable requirement. To begin, start your metronome at a medium tempo—about 80 bpm—and listen to it several different ways (either through its speaker or through headphones). Imagine that you are playing various instruments that are producing this click, for instance a woodblock with a hard rubber xylophone mallet or a drumstick. Sense the weight of the mallet/stick in your hand, and the approach to the beating spot of the woodblock, until you feel that you are actually playing the click. It might help to flex your wrist with your imaginary stick.

You might transfer the thought of the woodblock to a xylophone, a snare drum, or timpani, and then tap with each hand separately on your leg, chest, cheek, or table, first using only your fingers and then your whole hand. Tap your toes as well, concentrating on one foot at a time. At this point you would not necessarily be playing in a particular meter, merely with a string of pulses.

As you continue, try various combinations of hands and feet together, such as, in 4/4 meter the right hand and right foot both on beats 1 and 2, and the left hand and left foot together on beats 3 and 4. Try various combinations, such as maintaining the feet pattern and reversing the pattern for the hands. Also try these at a variety of dynamics, tempi, and meters—e.g., play in 5/4, only on the downbeats, or only on beat 2, or the "and" of 3, or on beat 4 set up four sixteenths, resting on the first one, etc. Challenge yourself in productive ways.

It is more difficult to maintain single pulses to a click than to subdivide (especially at a slow tempo), as the motor effect of two, three, four, or more parts to a beat seems to self-propel the time. Try practicing utilizing no beat subdivisions, gradually adding them on. If you are physically involved in time's motion (try walking in place and notice that your knees are moving on the half beat, feet as quarter notes, knees as eighth notes), then the mere act of preparing to play (arm or wrist in a timed motion, lifted on a pulse or subdivided part of a pulse that relates to your first note[s]) should help ground your time sense.

In preparing your pulse stew, I encourage you to invent your own exercises/studies/improvised gestures that incorporate a variety of playing surfaces, moving between sounds generated by hands/fingers and those produced by sticks/beaters and mallets. Wave a tambourine, articulate on its head, season with frame drums, world drums, "stick" drums, timpani, toys, mallet instruments etc. to flavor this dish. A banquet awaits. ➙●

The Elusive "Closed" Snare Drum Roll

Neil Grover

Centuries ago, my ancestors were the official bagel makers to the Czar. That should qualify me to say something about rolls! [*rimshot*] Seriously though, percussionists and drummers alike often have difficulty executing a silky smooth, consistent closed (aka: "buzz," "press," and "orchestral") roll.

INGREDIENTS:
A pair of good quality snare drum sticks
A drum pad or snare drum
A metronome
Patience
Time (not thyme)
A relaxed attitude

SERVES:
Concert percussionists, drummers, music educators.

I started out learning the open stroke rolls: 5-stroke, 7-stroke, and 9-stroke. My teacher was insistent that I develop strong hands with the ability to clearly articulate every double stroke. Like many young drummers, I spent hours practicing my open rolls, striving for the clarity of a machine gun! It was only after I mastered open rolls that I started my work on the closed roll, which I found far more difficult.

Unlike the open roll, the closed roll should sound legato and smooth with no discernable articulation. Imagine the sound of a fine concert violinist drawing the bow across a string, or an orchestral trombonist playing a long, sustained note. That uninterrupted body of sound is exactly the quality of sound that the closed snare drum roll emulates. The key qualities are sound that is consistent, smooth, and sustained. Sounds easy, but successfully executing this is quite another matter.

The first step in learning to play a quality closed roll is to relax. This is so important I'll say it again, *relax*! Some players call this roll a "press" roll, which actually is a misnomer. Pressing into the head is the last thing you want to do! Instead, you want to let gravity work for you and allow the sticks to fall into a "controlled bounce."

Here's how to combine the ingredients:

Step 1: Grip the sticks in a controlled, but relaxed manner, making sure your fulcrum is between the thumb and pointer finger.

Step 2: Working one hand at a time, allow each stick to strike the pad (or drum) and bounce as many times as possible until it naturally stops.

Step 3: Try Step 2 again, but this time experiment with releasing and adding pressure at the fulcrum. You should notice a change in the stick's rebound. Keep working at this, one hand at a time, until you achieve a consistent, even rebound with no less than four rebounds per stroke (the more the better).

Step 4: Using this "rebound" technique, play quarter notes, using alternate sticking at a slow tempo. Allow the sticks to "bounce" on the pad or drum. Keep working on this and try to keep one stick bouncing at all times (admittedly, very hard to do).

Step 5: At the same tempo, and being sure to allow the sticks to fully rebound, play, in sequence, four alternate-sticking quarter notes, eight eighth notes, twelve eighth-note triplets, and sixteen sixteenth notes. Repeat this pattern without stopping.

Step 6: Work on this exercise at increasing speeds with the goal of making every measure sound even and consistent. Ideally, at the optimum tempo, you should not hear the change of hands and the roll will sound continuous throughout the exercise (this could take many years to achieve). I strongly suggest practicing this exercise ten times without stopping.

After you have mastered the seven steps, I suggest this helpful visualization. Place the tips of both sticks down on the drum at the same time, imagining that the drum is a swimming pool filled with water. Lift up one stick at a time, imagining you are lifting your head out of the water for a breath of air. Alternating hands, allow each stick to drop down "into the water" letting it rebound many times. The concept is to envision the sticks in a state of constant "bouncing" motion, only lifting to "breathe." This is difficult and strange to do at first, but after some practice it provides an effective visualization for the successful execution of a closed roll.

Whatever you do remember: *be relaxed*! Tension has no place in the playing of a well-played closed roll. Some of the best orchestral snare drummers are the most relaxed when they play.

Now, who has those onion rolls? ➤

Cooking up a World Percussion Ensemble

Julie Hill

Infuse your music program with hot peppers by cooking up a world percussion ensemble that will baste your students and communities with a demi-glaze of passion, music appreciation, and education. *A cozinha ti chamar!* (The kitchen is calling you!)

This recipe works with any age group, from elementary school students through university percussion majors. When getting started, this epicurean delight can work with a limited shopping budget using commonly found ingredients already stored in your cupboard!

INGREDIENTS:
Vision and enthusiasm
Instruments currently in your music room
Musical arrangements

SERVES:
General music teachers, band directors, and percussion teachers of any age group wanting to diversify their musical kitchens and create an exciting, "cooking" show of their own.

Preparation
Why create a world percussion group in your music program? Students can certainly obtain a fantastic music education through "traditional" musical means. Why then explore diversifying your ensemble to incorporate world music?

By teaching world percussion in your music program to all students (no matter their primary instrument) you can broaden their educational experience while also generating enthusiasm for your band program as a whole.

I first tested this recipe from 1999–2002 as a middle school band director in the Murfreesboro (Tenn.) City Schools. Upon my arrival at my new job, I observed that few band students displayed enthusiasm for their instruments, the band, or learning music in general. I faced concerns that many of us do in that situation: disgruntled students, a lack of support from classroom teachers, and an administration not wanting to throw good money after bad.

I had to find a way to turn things around quickly so that I could look forward to going to work every day—or find another band-directing position.

The result: a world percussion ensemble that functioned as a part of my regular band class. Within a year, I had exploding student numbers, an excited and supportive community and administration, a budget for new instruments, and $20,000 in grants.

Instruments

Let's say you like the idea of creating a world percussion ensemble within your music program. What next? The first challenge is obtaining indigenous instruments.

The problem I ran into was that no one would provide me with the financial means to get started. There was no money to repair school-owned instruments, much less buy *conga drums*. In my attempt to discuss budgetary needs with my administration, I might as well have been speaking a foreign language, with notions of buying African *djembes* and Brazilian *surdos*. How then could I get started when I needed instruments to create the enthusiasm that would, in turn, facilitate the purchase of more instruments. It was a real Catch 22.

So, I thought about the percussion group Stomp and how it had been so successful in bringing novelty percussion music into the mainstream by utilizing everyday instruments. That is exactly what we did. I took my limited funds and purchased buckets and trash cans. Being a percussionist, I also brought in every instrument I had from home so that we could work on a limited number of hand drums and accessory instruments.

I next chose the most visible venue I could find, so that we could generate enthusiasm about our band program. I got my big break when each school in our district was asked to perform for a televised school board meeting. All the other band directors in the system performed traditional fifth- and sixth-grade tunes from their various method books.

My school had a reputation for having the worst band in the system, with 80 percent "at risk" students playing on school-owned instruments. Rather than try to perform equal repertoire using clarinets lacking pads, bells that would fall on the floor at random, and trumpets with perpetually sticking and dented valves, we decided (as a group) to do something completely different and see if we could grab the attention of our audience.

It worked like magic.

The evening of our debut performance finally arrived. I am sure that with our buckets, trash cans, and homemade items, our instrumentation seemed extremely unorthodox to the school board members and viewing audience. We performed two arrangements that involved Brazilian and African styles of percussion. In addition, the students all sang in Portuguese while they played the Brazilian *samba* arrangement. When we finished our performance, everyone in the room gave us a standing ovation. My students beamed with pride. We had done something good.

The positive results proved overwhelming. The next day I received numerous phone calls from school board members, administrators, and parents from other schools. The parents of my own students, normally disengaged and never present, began visiting my band room to see if they could help with anything. The music education supervisor for our school system paid me a visit and asked what resources I needed to service more students. Everyone wanted to know how we got the instruments, who wrote the musical arrangements, when we rehearsed, and more. When I told them that all of the instruments were mine or made by the students and that we had accomplished this on our own, everyone wanted to help. It was amazing to see how much support we received as a result of that one strategic performance. I suddenly had a budget to work with for my whole band program.

From this example, you can see that by using instruments already in your band room and by performing world percussion music in a high profile location, you can increase the support you receive for your music program as a whole.

Funding

The world music program that premiered before my school board that night continued to grow and became an after-school program, servicing three schools and more than 100 students per week and requiring four music teachers. I called the program Steel de Boro and performed a wide variety of world styles, primarily on steel pans. The group received $50,000 in grants from the BestBuy Music Zone (no longer in existence) and funding through various after-school programs. However, I continued to incorporate world percussion into my daily band program and will focus only on those aspects for the remainder of this recipe.

Many music programs have budgets for new instruments and repairs. If this is your situation, designate a portion of that for purchasing world percussion instruments.

Also, as in my case, remember that the people who allocate funding and designate music budgets often need a little taste of something before they will jump completely on board. You may have to make do with what you have for a limited time.

Many grants are available to help fund multi-cultural learning experiences in the classroom. Your state may also have an arts council grant for which you can apply. Identify the person in your school system who has a good knowledge of available grants. The Internet is also a valuable tool in searching for grants.

Instrumentation and Storage

Once you have the funds to purchase some instruments, no matter what size group you have, the important thing is to grow with a balanced instrumentation, purchasing instruments that will give you the greatest flexibility in learning a variety of styles. A balanced assortment from the following list is a good place to start:

- Bass drums or large drums: surdos, djun-djuns, or smaller bass drums.
- Medium to small drums: djembes, ashikos, timbaus, congas, or dumbeks.
- Metal sounds: cowbells, triangles, guiras.
- Wood sounds: Jam Blocks, claves, guiros.
- Assorted shakers.

Storage can be a concern depending on your rehearsal space. My band room in Murfreesboro was a double-wide portable shared by three teachers all working simultaneously. Creating shelving and using all vertical space provided a workable solution. Give every piece of equipment in your music room a home and a label. Students quickly will learn the names of the instruments, their correct spellings, and take great pride in caring for them if they know where they should be stored.

Musical Arrangements

I get numerous calls from music teachers asking where they can purchase arrangements of world percussion pieces. Many music publishers—Alfred Music, Innovative Percussion, and Row-Loff Productions to name a few—publish performable compositions in an array of styles and instrumentation. A well-known percussion group for young people, the Louisville Leopard Percussionists, has some fabulous published arrangements by leader Diane Downs (published by Hal Leonard).

Since all ensembles differ in size and ability level, I encourage you to consider making your own arrangements. Often, non-percussionists are hesitant to arrange world percussion pieces on their own, thinking they may mistake a cowbell on a recording for a brake drum. This is very common, but don't be afraid to try. Pull out some of your favorite world music compact discs and try to find one that lends itself to the instrumentation and ability level of your students.

If you have a wide variety of instruments, you can make substitutions. The first time I performed an arrangement of Brazilian pianist Sergio Mendes' "Magalenha," I didn't have a single traditional Brazilian percussion instrument in my band room. I carefully explained the instrument substitutions to the students so that they could always match every instrument with its country of origin, but that didn't limit our learning of repertoire or styles. I just made substitutions until we acquired the traditional instrument needed.

If you have questions about a particular sound or are unable to distinguish the division of parts, consult a percussionist in your area. He or she should be able to help.

Dessert
The positive results from incorporating world percussion into your music program are immeasurable. When asked if teaching world percussion takes away from valuable rehearsal time that could be spent on students' traditional band instruments, my answer is always a resounding "no." However, I also think that one must find the right balance in instructional time between world percussion and "traditional" band class; this differs by situation. In my own experience as a middle-school band director, students met five days per week. It was easy for me to dedicate one day a week (or, at certain times, two days) to world percussion and still maintain adequate student progress on traditional instruments.

Adding world percussion to your music program helps students become better rhythm readers, often one of the most common weaknesses in young music ensembles. By eliminating the variable of pitch, you can isolate and focus on rhythms, cultivating better rhythmic reading and ensemble groove. Both of these skills help students play more difficult repertoire when they go back to the traditional band rehearsal.

Students can experience improvisation at a very early age through world percussion. This helps alleviate the fear or hesitation for young people to improvise. Students will gain confidence while improvising on a non-pitched percussion instrument, which should then transfer to a student's traditional instrument. In a drumming ensemble, there are no wrong notes!

Another benefit of teaching world music is that students' practice time at home increases. By getting students excited about coming to band class and making music together, they are motivated to practice more at home on their traditional band instrument.

In teaching the cultural background of every musical style learned in world percussion sessions, you expose students to the geography, history, and social structure of countries throughout the world. This produces more tolerant, educated citizens while also garnering support from the traditional classroom teachers in your school. In some situations, you may be able to work with teachers from different disciplines to facilitate learning about the same geographical region. I have collaborated numerous times with the art teacher, general music teacher, and history teachers at schools in which I have taught. This can make for a powerful and fun learning environment for the students and teachers involved.

A final benefit of forming a world percussion group at any level is that the music performed is highly accessible to all types of audiences. This means higher attendance at concerts, more invitations to play in the community, and, if you are able to charge a fee, a means of generating or enhancing your current music budget.

Resources

The Percussive Arts Society (www.pas.org) is a valuable resource for any teachers aspiring to incorporate world percussion into their music program.

There are a number of places where instruments and music can be purchased at an affordable price. With a quick "Google" search, you can find just about anything you need in the percussion world.

I hope this recipe will inspire you and give you the confidence needed to incorporate world percussion into your music program. As a university percussion teacher now, I still see the benefits and results of teaching world percussion at any age. May your milk never curdle, may your larder be forever stocked! *Boa Sorte!* ➤

A Healthy Marimba Breakfast

Rich Holly

As a marimbist, at any given moment you may be called upon to perform as a soloist, in a recording session, in a chamber ensemble, or as a member of a large ensemble. Start each day with a healthy series of warm-ups that prepare you for any situation you might encounter and it will make each new performing experience more relaxing and enjoyable.

INGREDIENTS:
4 matched and lightly weighted marimba mallets
2 comfortable shoes
1 positive outlook
1 marimba, size to taste

SERVES:
Intermediate to advanced marimbists and other percussion keyboard players.

When working with students for the first time, either in a private lesson or a clinic setting, I always ask, "What is your warm-up routine?" All too often their response is along the lines of "Well...uh...I uh...," and it becomes clear they don't have a warm-up routine. Think of your daily warm-ups as breakfast: The best way to start your day is with a good, healthy warm-up routine.

I like to think that all marimba music contains one or more of the following types of playing: two-mallet scale-like passages, passages that contain leaps, and passages that contain double stops; and four-mallet passages consisting of block chords, mallet independence, one-handed rolls (double laterals), interval changes, and rolling. In addition, music sometimes goes up in pitch and sometimes goes down; sometimes the motion you need to make is parallel and sometimes it's contrary; and the rhythms you'll encounter can all be dissected into either duple or triple meter.

After you've stirred all this around, you should have a set of warm-ups consisting of one or more exercises for each type of technical playing, which are combined with the directions, motions, and rhythmic subdivisions you would come across in any possible performance setting.

As you develop your own set of exercises—which I strongly encourage, as they will be much more meaningful to you over the long haul—also keep in mind possible subcategories. For instance, there is not just one type of chord. Your four-mallet block chord exercise(s) should allow you to warm up using several chord types including major, minor, major 7th, dominant 7th, minor 7th, half diminished (minor 7th, flat 5), and fully diminished. As you become more comfortable with your exercises you can consider playing 9th chords while leaving out either the root or 5th. And, of course, chords are not always played in root position, so design your warm-up exercise to include all inversions, too.

A good warm-up session also includes time for you to observe yourself. Pay attention to your posture, your ability to be and remain relaxed, and how your entire body is moving as necessary at the marimba. Perform your warm-up exercises not necessarily for perfect note accuracy, but for warming up all the muscles that are required for performing, which includes muscles in the hips, abdomen, chest, and legs.

Before you perform each of your exercises, talk to yourself about which items you're expecting to pay attention to—which muscles you'll be concentrating on, which technique(s) you're about to utilize, what is the range of the exercise, and so on. After you perform each exercise, spend a few seconds recapping how it went—did you accomplish the *warm-up* aspect of the exercise, even though you may have missed a few of the notes? If you find that you are consistently hitting incorrect notes, take a few moments later that day to work on the exercise for the sake of accuracy, but during your warm-up routine, concentrate on, well, warming up.

While there are dozens of ways to design and arrange your warm-up exercises, here is one possible set of marimba warm-up exercises that would serve your needs:

- Two-mallet scales, played up and down for one octave in duple meter, followed by two octaves, and then followed by three octaves, all non-stop. Choose three starting pitches each day, and play all major and minor scales and modes that begin on each of those three pitches. Every four days you will have rotated through all possible scales and modes.

- Two-mallet arpeggios, played up and down in triple meter, alternating root position with all inversions, totaling a two-octave range. Establish a rotation of pitches and chord types (and continue to do that for all subsequent exercises).

- Two-mallet double-stops, played by starting with both mallets on any pitch and chromatically moving in contrary motion for a range of one octave, out and in, ending back on your starting pitch.

- Four-mallet block chords, played in close position, beginning with root position and followed up, and then down the instrument with all inversions in duple meter for a total range of three octaves.

- Four-mallet independence exercises, utilizing the 24 possible three- and four-mallet permutations in triple meter for the three-mallet permutations and duple meter for the four-mallet permutations. Hold any interval that is comfortable, and move up and down the instrument for a total range of three octaves. You definitely want a rotation established with these so they won't take you all day!

- One-handed rolls, played by holding four mallets, and working with a clear and rhythmic pattern in any meter so you know that you are in control of your wrist rotations. Speed up the exercise only when you can maintain rhythmic accuracy at the faster tempo.

- Interval changes may be performed either one hand at a time or with both hands simultaneously, and may alternate days between parallel and contrary motion. I particularly recommend that you develop several interval exercises.

- Four-mallet rolling. Find or arrange four to six "tunes" that you enjoy into chorales and use these on an alternating basis for your warm-up.

Just as with breakfast, we can't guarantee that each day we'll have enough time for a complete meal or warm-up. Instead of a cooked breakfast of an egg-white omelet, oatmeal, and a pot of coffee, some days you may only have time for a piece of toast and a glass of milk. Similarly, when you have days with less available time and are considering eliminating your warm-up routine, you'll be better served by having a quick yet effective start to your day. I recommend playing a two-mallet double-stop exercise that is either scale-based and/or arpeggio-based, followed by one or two four-mallet interval exercises. The double-stop exercise will touch on at least two of the three major techniques needed for that type of performance, and *all* four-mallet playing (regardless of independence-based, rolling-based, block chord-based, or what-have-you) uses interval changes.

I hope you keep your health in check by starting each day with a nutritious breakfast. Do the same for your marimba performance by starting each day with a healthy warm-up routine, and you'll be in the best performance shape possible. ➝●

Creative Practice

Steve Houghton

How many times have you gone into the practice room and ending up playing the "same old stuff" over and over? Oftentimes, it seems that drummers tend to practice more for fun than for truly learning the instrument. To really gain some skills on the drumset, you must come up with a solid practice routine, one requiring discipline and planning. At the same time, actual practice time may be at a premium and you must make every minute count, so I'm a fan of efficient practice as well.

INGREDIENTS:
Reading
Technique
Styles
Soloing

SERVES:
Drumset players at all levels

I've divided the practice routine into four main areas: reading, technique, styles, and soloing. I suggest that each area gets some attention at every practice session. Practicing only one or two of the areas leads to an uneven drummer. That being said, it is important to develop some materials that address all four areas at once, making for efficient practice.

Reading
Everyone enjoys a bargain and this is a good one! At first glance, this example looks like a typical reading exercise. While it can certainly help develop the player's reading skills, it can be so much more.

Play the exercise down top to bottom, reading the rhythms. Try using a metronome and increasing the tempo as you become more comfortable reading the exercise.

Technique
Next, play a ride cymbal beat over the top and play the rhythms with snare drum, bass drum, and then a combination of the two. This new coordination exercise will be a fundamental part of any drummer's technique.

1. Snare drum

2. Bass drum

3. Snare/bass combinations

Styles

You can also apply the rhythms to a samba groove.

Utilizing the same material, take the rhythms and put triplets underneath them (tripletize). While serving as a nice hand warm-up routine, it will now help to solidify the swing feel. The rhythms now being played in the swing style are laying the groundwork for chart reading and big band playing.

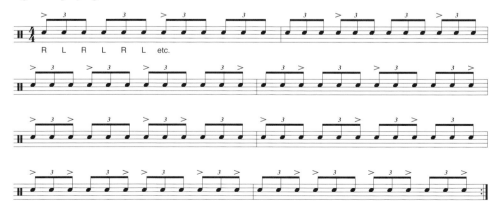

Different stickings can also be used, making it an even better technical exercise.

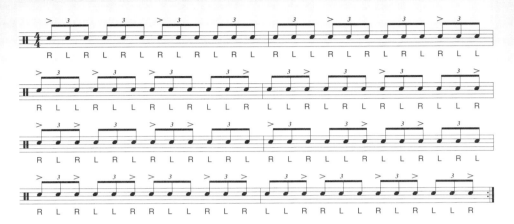

Soloing

Now play four bars of jazz time, then play line one of the reading with the triplet feel. Then play four bars of jazz time followed by line two with the triplet feel. You will now be "trading fours," which is an important solo format used in jazz performance.

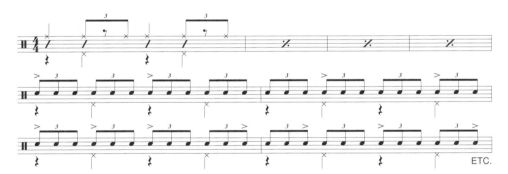

This recipe is a good example of how one can take almost any snare drum book and get multiple uses out of it with some creative practice ideas.

Good luck and have fun! ➤

Layering in a Rhythm Cake

Arthur Hull

This drum circle game not only educates the players in your circle about the importance of listening and dialog, but it is also a great way to get a solid groove started.

INGREDIENTS:

A drum circle with 15 to 30 players.

A full range of drums (low, medium. and high pitched) and percussion (bells, shakers and wood timbers) for melody lines to emerge out of the rhythm exchange that will take place.

SERVES:

Everyone in the percussion family. This recipe is appropriate for hand-drum players at any level of expertise, from beginning to advanced, and also works well in a circle that has participants with a mixture of levels of expertise.

Instructions

- The group will have their instruments at the ready.

- Designate a starting player. That person starts the rhythm song.

- Everyone else waits his or her turn to contribute.

- The person on the left of the starting player listens to the rhythm and then adds whatever rhythm he or she thinks would be appropriate to support, harmonize, or complement the rhythm being played.

- The person to the left of the second player listens to the rhythm song created by the two players, and then joins in by playing whatever rhythm he or she thinks would be appropriate to support, harmonize, or complement the rhythm being played.

- The next person in turn listens to the song as it is being created, and adds his or her rhythmical contribution to the piece.

- This process continues until all players in the circle have layered their rhythmical contribution into the composition and there is a complete rhythm song.

- After everyone has layered his or her part into the rhythm, and has enjoyed the composition for a while, the person who started that particular rhythm makes a call and leads a group rumble to a closing.

- The person to the left of the last starting player begins a new rhythm and continues this exercise.

- Everyone can take turns until everyone has had a turn starting a rhythm into which everyone else in the group layers. No two songs will be the same. Share your rhythmical spirit! ➤●

Teacher as Student as Teacher

Kalani

A formal education, in music or any other discipline, can be a rich and rewarding experience for both the teacher and the students, full of exhilarating and challenging moments. As an educator and a life-long student, my own experiences, even if from what seems like ages ago, are still offering me lessons and insights into my own learning process and helping me become both a better teacher and learner.

The purpose of this recipe is to identify, examine, and offer some strategies to help get the most out of the teacher-student relationship, no matter which hat you are wearing for the moment. In fact, the first principle to adopt is that we can all benefit from wearing both "teacher" and "student" hats at the same time.

INGREDIENTS:
Teacher spirit
Student spirit
Music spirit

SERVES:
All teachers and students

Teacher Spirit
Teaching is really a "leading out" of what is already inside the student. As teachers, we have a responsibility to offer a rich, well-planned, and thorough curriculum for our students. People come to us at great expense of both time and money. They deserve our highest standards and best efforts, but they also deserve something that is often filtered out in the institutionalized learning system: support in cultivating those characteristics that make them unique.

Formal curriculum often asks the student to simply reach for pre-set standards in knowledge, skills development, and performance. Of course, standards are important, and we must observe and measure the student's progress through tests and performance-based assessment. The difficult part can be looking beyond our personal or standardized goals and forming some kind of idea of the unique qualities and goals of the student.

Everyone brings to the table a rich background and an abundance of ideas. It's the responsibility of the teacher to identify, validate, and encourage those qualities that are within each student. One way we do this is by asking questions: "What kinds of music are you most interested in?" "Why are you passionate about your instrument?" "Do you improvise and/ or compose when you practice?" "What are your goals as a musician?" "What are your goals as a person?"

It's been my experience that teaching is more about asking the right questions than coming up with all the answers. "Teacher spirit" is about being more of a guide and supporter of the student, rather than a leader with the student trailing behind. A key concept that I identify in my book *Together in Rhythm* is one of "followership" as opposed to leadership. Followership is more of a partnership or agreement between two people who wish to move forward together. Rather than asking the student to jump through pre-defined hoops, empower them by celebrating their strengths and honoring their goals. This will help them feel capable and promotes full participation in the educational process. It may also create an atmosphere of mutual support and pride in your music program, because everyone feels like his or her opinions and desires matter. When we gain the ability to let go of our tendencies to want to control the students' approach to learning and simply let them grow into their authentic self, we embody the true essence of teaching and, as an added benefit, our job as teacher becomes effortless and more effective.

Student Spirit

A student is really a "self-teacher." As students, we sometimes expect our teachers to have all the answers. It's certainly true that many teachers have years of experience and knowledge that can help us benefit, but we must always remember that someone else's experience and knowledge is what has worked for them, but the same might not work for us.

We all learn in different ways and have different goals. Only you know what makes you most excited to get out of bed in the morning and run to your instrument to start practicing. Only you know why you are pursuing a career in music. And only you can ultimately be the best teacher for yourself. Knowing this and acting on your intuitions and instincts are two different things.

There's a lot of pressure to fit in and fall in line with pre-set curriculum and programs. I'm not suggesting that you rebel and refuse to do what's asked of you, but I encourage you to ask for what you want and need. This is your responsibility as a student. You can demonstrate "student spirit" by taking an active role in shaping your own education. You can demonstrate your involvement in your education by communicating with your instructor.

Consider the following statements and questions.

"I'm really interested in _____."

"How can we work more of _____ into my lessons?"

"Do you know of anyone who teaches _____?"

"My goal is to _____. How would you recommend I reach it?"

"I really feel drawn to _____ as a profession. What are my options?"

By maintaining an active approach to your own education, you not only help your teachers learn how they can help you (which often helps them become better teachers) but you form positive life habits, such as initiative and effective communication, which will transfer into your professional and personal life.

As a student, you deserve to have the education you are paying for, both in time and money. In some cases, you might feel as if you're working for your teacher, but in reality, your teacher is working for you! Keep in mind that if you don't shape your own education, someone else will shape it for you. If you're not sure what your goals are, create a list of things that excite and inspire you. Add to it over a period of days or weeks and eventually you will see a path emerge. Follow it with the help of all your teachers (inner and outer). When you stand in your own authenticity, you are at your best, and that honors all your teachers.

Music Spirit

All students become teachers (of themselves and possibly others), and hopefully all teachers will remain life-long students. I invite you to consider this view during your next lesson, while you are considering an educational program, and while you meet with friends and family. We all learn from each other all the time. It is only when we limit ourselves to one role or the other (teacher or student) that we miss out.

Becoming a compassionate teacher might involve becoming vulnerable and opening up to student feedback, while becoming a pro-active student might involve demonstrating more initiative or offering up your own plan. Approach your teacher with solutions, not problems. As long as we place the *spirit* of teaching and learning first and focus on working together to meet everyone's needs, we all benefit.

Set personal or institutional agendas aside and start asking questions—of yourself and each other. You might block out some time at the end of each lesson to discuss the effectiveness of the current curriculum. Is it moving in a mutually beneficial direction? What other resources are available outside of school? What areas need the most development and how can they be addressed? Is the student an effective learner? Does the student know how to set practice goals and reach them? What other factors are present in the student's life that could help or hinder progress?

When we take time to discover the person behind the label (student or teacher) and travel down the path of learning together, we come closer to reaching our potential for growth and gain more satisfaction from the process.

Perhaps the greatest gift teachers can give students is to instill them with the confidence to express themselves, and the tenacity to look past would-be critiques and be guided by their own intuition. The best testament to any teacher is a successful student—a student who is embodying his or her authentic-self and being the best musician (and person) he or she can be. ➤●

A Multiple-Percussion Approach to Drumset

Glenn Kotche

One can expand the musical possibilities of the drumset by taking a multiple-percussion, or total percussion, approach to both setup and playing.

INGREDIENTS:
A small amount of basic drumset skill.
A dash of familiarity with, and playing ability on, other instruments and techniques in the percussion family.
A modest amount of ripened desire to challenge oneself physically and mentally.
A heaping amount of musical curiosity and an open mind.

SERVES:
Drumset players at all levels.

The drumset needn't be a codified configuration of specific instruments: bass drum, snare drum, a couple of toms, one cymbal for riding, another for crashing, and some hi-hats. The sole purpose of the drumset performer doesn't have to be that of a strict timekeeper within the styles of groove-based music. Instead, the drumset or drumkit can be viewed as exactly that: a malleable kit comprising a grand array of sounds and possibilities from which this instrument was originally conceived.

The drumset can be viewed the same way as a concert multiple-percussion setup: an instrument that incorporates many different colors from the percussion family using the unique techniques inherent of those various instruments. (The only technical difference between concert multi-percussion and drumset is that the latter incorporates both the hands and feet.) Keeping time—as important and fun as it can be—is only one function of percussion in the full breadth of music.

This instrument is a very young one and has a lot of possibilities. Let's not think of the drumset as separate from the rest of the percussion family. Instead, let's utilize all that we've learned in our other non-drumset percussion studies to help broaden this instrument's palette.

This recipe has been passed down for generations from the forefathers of our instrument. To gain some perspective on this approach, we have to provide a pinch of history.

According to the legendary Max Roach, the drumset is the original multiple percussion and multi-cultural instrument. It was first approached this way with the late 19th/early 20th-century practice of double drumming. This was a precursor to the drumset, where the bass drum (sometimes with a small cymbal attached to it) and snare drum were played simultaneously using drumsticks. The multi-racial aspect comes from both the influence of European style regimental music—which was common after the Civil War—and the influence of African-derived music that was becoming more common in urban areas of the United States—especially New Orleans. The instruments used and rhythmic ideas (such as syncopation) incorporated into these styles collectively informed the music, which would eventually grow to become jazz and rhythm & blues.

Thanks to the invention of the bass drum pedal and exposure to ethnic instruments from other cultures, the drumset began to take shape. The first modern versions in the 1920s not only included European-style bass drums, snare drums, and early relatives of the hi-hat, but also Chinese tom-toms and cymbals, Turkish cymbals, African tom-toms, home-grown woodblocks and cowbells, and various other sounds effects or "traps" (contraptions), which were common in silent movie houses and vaudeville shows at the time. This truly was an instrument comprising multiple, individual percussion flavors combined together in a new and unique way.

The drumset expanded in the 1930s with drummers such as Chick Webb and Sonny Greer incorporating mallet percussion, timpani, chimes, and gongs into their large theater setups to accompany the growing big bands of the era. Ever since, the idea of broadening the sonic palette of the basic drumset has existed. The popularity of this approach is constantly in flux, and the concept has evolved with changing musical styles as well as improvements in percussion manufacturing and technology.

For this feast let us focus on three distinct dishes. Our appetizer is allowing the possibility of any percussion instrument to be incorporated into the drumset. Our side dish will be employing a variety of implements and performance techniques from which to coax succulent sounds from these instruments. And the main dish is a bountiful array of ways to support, guide, flavor, and spark the music we're making.

I can assure you that this recipe is not intended solely for the experienced and active drummer who has a variety of diverse performance outlets and the freedom to incorporate new things, but is also practical and important for the student drummer who is still honing his or her craft through lessons, school ensembles, and hours in the practice room.

Following are some simple and practical suggestions for how to introduce, become familiar with, and integrate this percussive recipe into the full menu of what you, as a drummer, are able to contribute to the music you make. These are just initial exercises that should serve as catalysts for ideas of how to further develop physical ability. They should also give an idea of some of the musical capabilities and options that we have—choices that will enable us to better serve the music.

Step One
Take any piece of easy snare drum music and move one hand to a different surface on your set. After playing it this way, substitute a maraca for a stick in one hand. Pay close attention to the balance between the hands both in volume and tonal color. Changing things up like this can also affect the timing of the preparatory stroke or the qualities of the rebound. All of these considerations should be assessed and factored into the performance of the music.

Next, exchange the maraca for a brush and slide every note instead of using a stroke. Again, factor in adjustments that you'll need to make to properly execute the music. Keep experimenting with various combinations of implements, surfaces, and pieces of music. This idea can train you to be able to incorporate more than one sound at a time when the music might call for it.

Step Two

Take a piece of music from a band method book written for two or three players—for example: the snare part of a band song with the accompanying bass drum and cymbal parts. First, make sure you can play each part separately. Next, play just the bass drum and cymbal (now hi-hat) parts simultaneously using only your feet. Finally, try playing all three parts together, treating your body as the full percussion section.

If this proves difficult at first, attempt one measure at a time, breaking it down into combinations of two limbs before incorporating all three, repeating each measure several times. Eventually, combine two or more measures into short phrases. Then attempt several lines in a row until you get used to reading the three parts together. It's important to note that reading multiple lines of music is a key requirement for contemporary concert multiple-percussion performance.

This is an exercise not only in independence but also in ensemble playing by treating our bodies as microcosms of a percussion section—a section capable of providing the meter, rhythmic direction, formal cues, punctuations, and dashes of sonic color.

Step Three

Using a simple snare drum duet commonly found in snare drum method books, play it as a duet between the right and left hands. (It can also be quite useful to slow it down and try it between other possible limb combinations as well: right hand and right foot, left hand and left foot, right foot and left foot, etc.)

After this, position an orchestra bell kit on one side of the drumset. Assign one hand to play one part on bells and the other hand to play the other part on snare drum. At first, just pick one pitch on the bells—let's say C. The next step is to choose two pitches—C and G—and alternate between them every other line, effectively adding melody to a monotone part. Next, try alternating pitches every other measure. Once some comfort has been reached with this arrangement, pick a scale—C Major—and play each successive note in that hand's written part as the ascending and descending C Major scale.

For more advanced players, the hand playing snare drum can then be orchestrated around the set, as well as adding feet ostinatos. Eventually, execute simple melodies with one hand while the other three limbs accompany on other instruments in your set. This will allow you to contribute not only rhythmically, but also melodically or harmonically when appropriate.

Step Four

Pick a drumset beat *du jour*; any standard rock groove will do. Play each backbeat, which would normally be played on snare drum, on a different surface each time. You can even develop a pattern: snare, rack, floor, repeat. Every so often, move the ride/hi-hat part to a different surface like the cymbal bell, floor-tom rim, mounted tambourine, cymbal stand, mounted woodblock, or cowbell, etc. Then make those orchestrations occur more frequently, in turn creating a sort of melody.

For example: with eight eighth notes in a measure of 4/4, think of orchestrating the first three (counts "1 & 2") on the ride cymbal, moving from the bell toward the edge, then the fourth ("&" of "2") on the floor-tom rim, the fifth note ("3") on the floor-tom head, the sixth ("&" of "3") on its rim again, repeating this pattern (head and rim) for the seventh and eighth notes ("4 &").

More advanced players can even substitute some of the rests in the snare part (or backbeat), filling in the part with notes on the snare rim, mounted tambourine, or any other surface.

This exercise can illustrate the melodic possibilities inherent within a standard rock beat. Ideally though, this will enable the drummer to orchestrate beats in a way that might better suit the music or even flavor the music in a way to give it a fresh sound and energy.

There have been drummers from every style and time period of contemporary music who have approached the drumset in a total-percussion way. We've already seen a historical overview of how various percussion instruments have been incorporated into the drumset. Some more contemporary introductions include: jingles mounted on hi-hats; foot-operated cowbells or woodblocks; mountable bongos and other ethnic drums; and, of course, electronic drums and drum triggers.

The multiple percussion drumset doesn't need to be large and difficult to transport. To the contrary, instruments can be chosen for their broad applicability; using an assortment of implements on a few instruments can yield an abundance of sounds and choices. Following are some additional considerations on how we can bring various concepts, techniques, and tools into the realm of drumset.

I've already mentioned the idea of treating the drumset as a microcosm of the percussion section. One great example of this is the conversion of parts from a Latin American percussion section to the various voices of the drumset as embodied in Western adaptations of samba, bossa nova, and mambo, to list a few. Another example is using multiple stick or mallet grips on drumset to achieve a different attack or to execute one-handed rolls like those common in vibraphone and marimba performance.

Keep in mind, too, that all the members of a percussion section aren't always playing. Just because it's part of your drumset doesn't mean it has to make an appearance in every song. Don't be afraid to let only one voice speak at a time. Keep the option open of switching between various instruments and implements at different points appropriate to the music.

I like to consider the percussionist's role in an orchestra. An orchestral percussionist may need to count copious amounts of rests just to get to one big triangle roll, suspended cymbal swell, or tambourine accentuation. The composer intended these unique colors to be utilized for specific musical effects. The various instruments, implements, and techniques available to drumset players can be used for keeping time, but they can also be used for coloristic and textural purposes. We can provide a contrast to other parts in the ensemble or help illustrate lyrics. We can create a chaotic musical atmosphere or provide a tone and rhythm that pulls the rest of the music together and provides focus for the whole.

Historically, drummers have used many types of implements on the drumset. A classic example is brushes. Originally fly swatters, they were employed on drums not only for a softer, gentler striking tool but to also slide on the drumhead, creating a sound akin to sandpaper blocks. Timpani mallets were used much in the same way that they were intended except on different surfaces. They allowed drummers to create long, sustained tones by rolling on toms and cymbals.

Other implements have also been taken out of their original contexts and incorporated on drumset. Some of these include chopsticks, marimba and keyboard percussion mallets, triangle beaters, coins, violin bows, Hawaiian puili sticks, knitting needles, Super Balls, broom bristles, and even kitchen utensils. These, along with homemade sticks and mallets (I construct my own spring-tipped threaded metal dowels), give us many ingredients with which to spice up the music.

However, it's not just the tools, it's how you use them. The drumstick alone can produce a multitude of tones from a single drum by playing different parts of the drum (edge, rim, shell), using different parts of the stick (cross-stick, stick shot) and using various strokes (dead strokes, buzzes).

Let us even consider using other percussion instruments as beaters. I love riding on the floor tom with a maraca or small sleighbells. A common practice is to play a shaker or tambourine with one hand while the other hand plays the drums with a stick. Wrist and ankle bells can also be used to great effect. Some drummers have abandoned sticks altogether and utilized hand drumming techniques to coax diverse sounds out of the drums.

In closing, I've found the practice of throwing any and all percussion knowledge, experience, and abilities into a blender and creating an approach of total percussion on the drumset extremely practical and valuable. By not thinking of the drumset as separate from the rest of the percussion family, drumset performers can view themselves as true percussionists whose functions and capacities are extensive—not singularly prescribed.

Think of the drumset as a multiple percussion setup with limitless possibilities in the combination of instruments and implements that it is composed of. The exceptional nature of the drumset allows us to expand the parameters of the percussionist's capabilities and possibilities. Percussion, in its many broad roles and attributes throughout the breadth of music, can serve as an example for the future development of the drumset and drumset performance. ➤●

Making Your Compass

Lalo

Thoroughly assessing your goals can help you to optimize the time you invest in your career. This recipe guides you through identifying your ambitions and further aids you in determining the best path to achieve them. The result of the process outlined below is an infusion of conviction, direction, and motivation to your music as well as your daily routine.

INGREDIENTS:
Paper
Pen

SERVES:
Artists of all levels.

By the time I was in college, whenever someone asked me my career goals, I was able to give a very clear, definite answer: I wanted to tour as a performing vibraphonist playing my original compositions. And when he or she further inquired about the specifics of what set me apart from the other artists who wished to accomplish the same thing, I explained that I planned to expose the listening world to my instrument in a new and contemporary setting. This meant writing and performing music that was fresh and relevant, yet also managed to showcase and realize the possibilities of the vibraphone. I was firm, determined, and willing to work hard. I knew where I wanted to go. So how was I to get there?

Berklee College of Music provided many helpful tools, but I believe that I would have gotten even more out of school if I had regularly looked up my path to see where I was currently headed in relation to where I wanted to go. For instance, while at Berklee I found that it's easy to be in such a hurry to progress that one neglects to learn things deeply. Mike Mainieri calls this (learning a lot of things a little bit) the "buffet" approach. How can you firmly plant your foot on the next step up the ladder if your toehold is slippery?

I'm not attempting to advocate close-mindedness or downplay the value of adventurousness (the exposure to so many different kinds of music at Berklee positively influenced my playing), I'm just encouraging diligence in assessing how one's current actions will likely affect where one is headed. I had the design for my compass in mind but wasn't utilizing its full potential.

Recently, my friend Stefon Harris reminded me how important it is to make your own compass, follow its guidance, and update it when necessary. He was also exceedingly helpful in breaking down the steps of the process. When I recently reassessed my aims I discovered that I had accomplished many of my old goals, and some of my past aspirations were no longer important to me while several new ones had arisen. In its entirety, my new compass was different than my old one and pointed me on a slightly, but significantly, divergent path. As a result, I adjusted my daily practice routine (as well as my business practices) to optimize my time and better fit my revised objectives.

STEP ONE: Gather the tools
Figure out what moves you. What brings you joy? Why do you play music? How do you like to spend your time?

STEP TWO: Choose your features
Decide what you want to do with your life. What are your life-long aspirations/career goals?

STEP THREE: Design your compass
Break it down. Where do you want to be in fifteen years? Five years? Three months?

STEP FOUR: Calibrate
How do you get there? What musical steps do you need to take in order to reach your goals? Look at your three-month goal and decide how to accomplish it through your practice routine and any other necessary steps. Focus on manageable, concrete goals for the short-term that most directly lead you toward your long-term goals.

The steps of the process may sound easy, but they require a great deal of commitment and honesty. I've found that the first answer that comes to mind when encountering these questions may be an outdated response (a remnant from the last time you thought things through), an attempt to overcompensate for what you perceive as your weaknesses (focusing on immediate obstacles rather than first clarifying your long-term goals), or too broad of an answer to be useful. Writing out each step is necessary in order to more thoroughly compose your thoughts and to have a guidebook for the future; it's also great motivation for staying on track with your commitment.

Educator/performer Hal Crook once told me that it takes practice to learn how to practice. Think of this time as an investment in learning how to practice more optimally. Everyone's process of divining their goals and how to achieve them will be different, but if you put in the time and effort the ultimate result will be the ability to craft a more direct path to your aspirations. Conviction is also a natural result of this process, and I find that knowing where my steps are leading me adds confidence to my playing and enthusiasm to my practice. ➤●

Good Drum Circles Are Not Just "Pot Luck"

Rick Mattingly

The great drum circle facilitator Arthur Hull always advises those who aspire to lead such events not to turn the drum circle into a drumming class, and he's right. The basic principle behind all drum circles is that of establishing a sense of community, similar to the feeling people get when they sing together, and there should be plenty of room for freedom of expression. It's not a classical percussion ensemble performance with specific, assigned parts; it's a celebration united by rhythm.

But staying with the comparison to singing, imagine telling a group of people that each of them can sing whatever they want—all at the same time. The result wouldn't be very musical, and wouldn't create much sense of community, either. People need some fundamental structure in order to sing together, and taking a few moments to acquaint them with the words and melody of a song doesn't constitute turning the sing-along into a music class.

Likewise, one should always have a "recipe" when leading a drum circle.

INGREDIENTS:

A group of people who may or may not have ever played drums before
A set of simple rhythmic phrases that can be easily taught
A flexible attitude

SERVES:

Any type of community drum circle

People often assume that the easiest way to get people to do something is to tell them that they can do whatever they want. But unlimited freedom often paralyzes people because there are too many possibilities. Most folks like to be given some kind of framework, along with the option of filling in that framework however they want.

The more experience people have with drumming, the less framework they need. For instance, when drum circles are held at Percussive Arts Society conventions, just about everyone there is an accomplished drummer, and so the facilitator can start a basic rhythm, or even just a pulse, and the participants will have the experience and knowledge to play something that fits, and they also know to keep their ears open and to react to what is being played around them.

But a PASIC drum circle is the exception, not the norm. In most situations, although you might have some people there who can jump right in and play something appropriate with little or no preparation from the facilitator, there are likely to be other people there who are new to this type of playing environment. Perhaps they have never played a drum (or any instrument) before, or perhaps they have played, but it's always been very structured. They've never been given permission to "just play," and they don't know how to apply what they know.

This is where the facilitator does his or her job, which is to help people participate (and then to get out of the way and let them run with it).

Start by laying down a few general ground rules. These might include explaining different gestures you will make during the drumming; e.g., this means get softer, that means get louder, this means stop, that means start back up, this means get faster, and so on. Just about every facilitator I've ever seen has done this. The trouble is, some of them stopped with that.

Just as a song leader would want to make sure that everyone knows at least some of the words (even if just the chorus), a drum circle facilitator should give people a basic rhythmic vocabulary to work with. There are a variety of ways to do this, but I am going to share just one that has worked for me in several situations.

I borrow a technique I learned in an elementary music class. I go around the room, ask each person's name, and teach the group to play each person's "name pattern." (If not everyone knows everyone else, this in itself is a good start to creating a community feeling.) Then we start combining names. I'm pretty sure that in every group I've ever done this with, there was at least one person whose first and last names were each one syllable (e.g., Jim Brown, Ben Smith), so that makes a good quarter-note pulse. Then there will be someone with a two-syllable first name and a one-syllable last name (e.g., Susan Peak, Michael Carr), so that gives us two eighths and a quarter to play over the quarter-note pulse. Then I'll look for a one-syllable first name and a two-syllable last name, which gives us a quarter and two eighths pattern. Two-syllable first and last names gives us straight eighths.

At that point, I divide the class in half (e.g, Ben's group and Susan's group). We'll then try different combinations of people's name rhythms in the group. I start out with names that can be played with just quarters and/or eighths, but as the group gets comfortable with that, I go to names that might involve sixteenths and/or syncopation. But I keep everything in 2/4 time and avoid triplets so that every pattern works with every other pattern.

Often there will be more than one person with the same pattern. I usually put them together into mini-groups who share a rhythm. If quite a few people have the same rhythm, I'll sometimes ask one of them for a middle name instead of a first name, and sometimes we will do first, middle, and last names depending on the number of syllables involved. With advanced groups I've had combinations of 2/4 name patterns and 3/4 name patterns, so that the rhythms sort of "revolve" around each other, but with less experienced groups I always keep all of the patterns in 2/4. I will also use longer or shorter versions of names for rhythmic variety, such as Tom or Thomas, or Nick or Nicholas. A middle initial can also add flavor to a name rhythm.

Once we've been through a reasonable amount of two-name/rhythm combinations, I divide the group into three sections and we start mixing and matching the patterns that way. Depending on the size of the group, we might go to four, five, or six patterns at a time. If the group has a variety of instruments, it's good to have different sounds for each rhythm; e.g., one rhythm on drums, another on woods (woodblocks, claves, rhythm sticks), and another on metals (cowbells, triangles). Drums can be divided into large drums and small drums, as well as into bass sounds and rim sounds. If you have experienced djembe or conga players, they can do slaps.

Ultimately, I have each person play his or her own pattern, with all patterns being played at once. Often, it helps to start one person off (the quarter-note pulse name), and then add each person one at a time, playing each person's pattern with him or her until you are sure they are locked in. Once they get going, let them enjoy it for a while, but keep your eye on everyone, and if someone gets off, help them get back into it. Once they are locked in, I lead them in things like speeding up and slowing down, getting louder and softer, and so on.

Then we stop for a few minutes (as much as anything to give everyone's hands a rest), and I tell everyone to pair up with someone in the group and trade names. (If there is an odd number of people in the group, I join in and trade with one of them). I give them a few minutes to teach each other their rhythm and to practice, and then we all play together again, but with each person playing someone else's name pattern.

After we've played that for a while and everyone is comfortable playing a couple of different rhythms and locking in with the group, I invite them to get creative with the patterns they know. I give them options such as: play your first name and some else's last name (or vice-versa); combine your first name with someone else's first name (or use two last names); just play your first or last name over and over; make a longer pattern by playing your name, then another name, back and forth. I also tell them that they don't have to play the same thing all the time; they can play their own name a few times, then switch to another name, then mix and match the names, and so on. I also tell them that they do not have to limit themselves to the two names they've practiced; they can play any name pattern in the group.

People who are new to this type of thing will often stay with one name throughout, and that's fine. People who have more experience, or who are simply more adventurous, will often go from one pattern to another, and that's fine, too. I always tell the people that the important thing is blending with the group pulse. It doesn't matter that much what each person plays as long as it all fits together. So if someone is more comfortable just laying down the pulse, that's fine because that pulse helps keep everyone together.

We all start playing again, and this is our longest playing section and the most fun. Often, I'll be the one playing the basic pulse so that the group members can experiment with different patterns. I'll also lead some of the typical drum circle "games" by signaling for different groups to drop out from time to time (e.g., I'll let just the drums play, then just the metals, then just the woods, then have different combinations of sounds play together), or by signaling for everyone to play very softly and then leading them in hitting a certain accent together (it's usually best to start with accenting the downbeat), or by getting faster, and so on. We typically bring it to a climax where rhythm patterns are forgotten and everyone is playing as loud and fast as possible, and then we literally end with a big, unison bang.

It's not a "drum class" by any means, in the sense that I'm not teaching an African, Latin, or any other kind of "authentic" rhythm. But it's not a free-for-all, either, because there is a specific set of rhythms that everyone is drawing from. And once everyone is comfortable with those rhythms, they are free to mix and match them however they want, so there is plenty of freedom.

With smaller groups, you can probably play every name pattern in the group. With larger groups, you might have to just pick out a few that work well. You could also use famous names, in which case you can pick a theme, such as American Presidents: James Polk, John Adams, Franklin Pierce, Abraham Lincoln, George Washington, John Quincy Adams, and so on. It doesn't have to be people's names; it can be any set of words. (If you are doing this in a school and can tie your theme into something they are studying, the teachers will love you!)

You can also teach a set of rhythms through call-and-response or "echoing." The point is, give the group some raw material to work with. Rather than inhibiting them, it will free them up to be creative within a framework and will prevent your drum circle from being a cacophony of people just banging away with wild abandon. Give them a specific set of ingredients to work with, and your musical stew will have a much better flavor. ➤●

A Good Practice Session Should be Like a Four-Course Meal

William Moersch

I have heard it said that we should practice every day that we eat. This is excellent advice—that practicing should become as integral a part of our daily routine as eating, but it begs the question, "How should we practice?"

Success in life is often dependent on the outcome of many unforeseen events, but some of the most common traits of successful people are organization, preparation, and having clear goals. A successful practice regimen requires the same type of clear objectives. This, then, is a discussion of productive practice organization.

INGREDIENTS:
Appetizer
Main course
Salad
Dessert

SERVES:
All percussionists

Appetizer: Warm-up
A good warm-up routine is essential to productive, safe practice. I usually begin by soaking my hands, wrists, and forearms in warm water, as hot as I can comfortably stand, for several minutes. Then, I gently stretch the same areas, slowly working through a range of motion. (For a more complete discussion of this and other physical issues, see Dr. Darin Workman's book, *The Percussionists' Guide to Injury Treatment and Prevention*.)

Following the purely physical portion of the warm-up, I like to play a variety of musical warm-up exercises, such as slow, steady rhythms, legato tones, or scale patterns. Another important factor in my routine is to involve some aspect of mental concentration along with the physical motion to warm up the brain as well as the muscles. Sequential or modulating patterns are very good for this, especially those that require you to think ahead of what your hands are doing. I often use a sequence of mode scales, playing a series of eight modes on a single tonic note, ascending in one mode and descending in the next, and then gradually modulating the entire pattern through all twelve keys.

Main Course: Principal Objective
Once you are warmed up, limber, and alert, move to the principal task for the practice session. This might involve learning new repertoire, fixing problems in repertoire currently in

preparation, or simply addressing a particular technical challenge. However, this principal objective should be clearly determined before you begin. Try to set daily goals that are within your grasp, neither too easy nor too difficult. There should always be a sense of accomplishment for one day's achievements and still a sense of positive anticipation toward the next day's challenge.

As you practice, be as thoughtful and organized in your approach to the task as possible. Fully consider both the musical structure and the component parts of what you are working on and be creative in addressing each aspect. Larger projects may require careful analysis and division into smaller portions, even to the point of creating a daily or weekly schedule for the successful and timely completion of each segment. Complex, multi-layered music may require working on separate layers individually, becoming completely familiar with each part alone, before attempting to put them all together.

Be conscious of identifying the most important material, whether simply melody versus harmony or principal voice versus accompaniment, and seek to make the balance correct. Always work within the musical structure and phrases of the piece, being careful not to put breaks in arbitrary places, such as page turns that occur in the middle of phrases. Any non-musical breaks that you learn in practice will be that much harder to smooth over later. An excellent aid to productive practice is to regularly record yourself and listen back with as much of an objective viewpoint as possible. Is what you think or want to have happen musically actually and noticeably happening?

I am a strong advocate of slow, careful, accurate practice. Play something only as fast as you can play it correctly with all rhythms, pitches, dynamics, and phrasing. When you can play it consistently at that tempo, gradually increase the tempo in small increments, reinforcing the same degree of accuracy at each level of tempo increase. If you begin to make mistakes, slow down and try to isolate exactly why you are making the mistake. Check for large motion errors by "air" playing. If you are seeking to perform from memory, test your memory away from the instrument, through visualization or by attempting to write the music out. The key principle is that perfect practice makes perfect performance; anything less and you are just training yourself to make mistakes.

Musical creativity is another important skill to develop during your practice sessions. Although there are many aspects to this subject, one approach that I have found extremely useful over the years, especially for a solo instrument, is to think of orchestrating color. By this, I mean to imagine which instruments of the orchestra might be playing various parts of the music and with what types of orchestral color. Then, strive to match that wide range of orchestral timbre on your individual instrument.

Salad: Sight Reading (because it's GOOD for you)
Every practice session should include a portion of sight-reading practice. Reading music is no different than reading language. The process is exactly the same: learning individual symbols for sounds (letters, rhythmic values, pitches); then learning standard combinations of those symbols and sounds (words, rhythms, scales and chords); then taking in larger chunks of information whole rather than as individual symbols (phrases, sentences, melodic or harmonic structures); and, finally, developing the ability to predict what is coming next based on context.

To work on sight-reading, you need a collection of level-appropriate material. I use everything from old snare drum or keyboard method books, taken at a significantly faster tempo than indicated (e.g., in "two" or "one" instead of the original "four" or "three"), and various etude collections for other instruments (e.g., flute, violin, trumpet), to specific sight-reading or sight-singing texts. A graded sample of such material might be: Hering's *Etudes in all the Major and Minor Keys for Trumpet*, Hering's *Twenty-Eight Melodious and Technical Etudes*, Berkowitz, Fontrier and Kraft's *A New Approach to Sight Singing*, Bona's *Rhythmical Articulation*, Dufresne & Voisin's *Develop Sight Reading* (and the G. David Peters transcription, *Develop Sight Reading for Snare Drum*), and Cirone's *Portraits in Melody*.

The most common professional situation requiring sight reading is in an ensemble setting, whether a rehearsal, performance, or recording session. In that context, the principal rule is *do not stop*. Far worse than missing a note or two is stopping or getting lost. Therefore, all sight-reading practice should be geared to this end.

A basic primer in the proper method of practicing sight-reading is as follows. First, glance over the entire excerpt, looking both for basic roadmap information and, in particular, for anything you have not seen before (e.g., a new rhythm, a new scale or harmony, an unusual structural issue). Then, choose a musically appropriate tempo and play from beginning to end, getting as much of the material as accurately as possible. Do not start and stop, back up, or turn the time around. If you get into trouble, lay out for a beat or two, but come back in at the right place. Train your eyes to read ahead of your hands, often a full measure or more, depending on the complexity of the material.

It is important to find material that is suitable for your level of ability. After reaching the end of the excerpt, consider how you did. Did you get 30% correct, or 60%, or 90%? If 30% or less, this material is too difficult for your level and you need to find easier material to start with. If 90% or more, the material is too easy for your level and you need to increase the challenge. If 60% (just right!), then look back at whatever gave you trouble. Do not actually play anything out of context, just look at it again and figure out what you missed. Then, play the entire excerpt again, from beginning to end. Go on to the next page and, eventually, the next book. Never play through a sight-reading excerpt more than once or twice in a row; it's not sight-reading after that. Have a large enough stack of material so that you will have forgotten everything by the time you come back to it again.

Dessert: Repertoire Review
The final component of a successful practice session is the dessert, the reward for doing all of that hard work. This is the time for you to remind yourself of the sheer joy of playing music, the reason that all of this daily effort is ultimately rewarding. Play through a piece that is already in your repertoire and just enjoy the act of making music. Look forward to the day when that difficult piece in progress becomes just another part of your continuing repertoire.

Good luck with your practicing and *bon appétit!* ➤

Focused, Result-Oriented Practice Sessions

Jeff Moore

This is a recipe for creating efficient, purpose-driven practice sessions that will result in consistent growth and improvement over time. It is a recipe that many performers have shared with one another, and it has helped many percussionists realize their performance goals. One great "chef," Dr. Steve Hemphill of Northern Arizona University, was good enough to share his practice recipe with me and I found it to be quite satisfying. It is important to follow the recipe accurately and to frequently assess your results through performance and video/audio recordings.

INGREDIENTS:
1. One journal or notebook. Use this book to record short-term and long-term goals, along with notes and observations from each practice session. You can record your teacher's and your own ideas for incremental sequential learning strategies. For example, consider how you propose to break down a large goal (e.g., learning a piece of music or groove) into smaller goals that correspond with the time scheduled for each practice session.
2. Have your requisite practice materials (e.g., stick or mallet bag, books, music, recording devices, etc.) handy and in one location nearby, so you begin each practice session fully equipped.
3. A clock or watch to time your "practice to break" ratio. Fifty minutes of practice to ten minutes of break is recommended, but each individual will determine what feels the best. The clock should also be used to ensure that practice sessions commence at roughly the same time each day, if possible. Maintaining a consistent practice schedule and routine is key to maximizing practice results. The body and brain will become conditioned to accept the information more readily, and a routine establishes the discipline required in continuing long-term improvement and growth.

SERVES:
All percussionists, regardless of instrument focus and experience.

A Recipe for Perfect Practice
1. Begin with a good, relaxed warm-up. Slowly and methodically stretch the muscles that will be used. Focus your attention frequently on the arms, wrists, and fingers. Do not neglect the legs, feet, back, and neck as tension can inhibit a smooth flowing performance and contribute to a feeling of exhaustion. As Chef Hemphill said, "Good posture, relaxation, and physical flow can be enhanced by awareness of the breathing."

2. Immediately following the warm-up, begin the practice session with a familiar piece, pattern, or song that can be played comfortably.

3. Following the familiar piece, one can begin to go on to the more unfamiliar (some would say "difficult") work. To me, difficulty is a matter of familiarity. The more familiar you are with material, the easier you perceive it to be. Consistent, organized practice sessions help you gain familiarity with new material more quickly. It is important to begin the "unfamiliar" immediately after the "familiar" so you can compare the relaxation and flow between the two tasks. A goal would be to maintain the same feeling and relaxation as you go from the familiar to the unfamiliar.

4. In order to maintain this feeling of relaxation and flow, slow and careful practice is necessary. Many times we practice material much faster than we can play it accurately and cleanly. Every time we make mistakes due to practicing too fast, the mistakes are being learned. Practice only at a tempo that results in correct performance. Increasing the tempo is a matter of repetition, once the material has been learned and internalized correctly and without mistakes. Prior to a performance, I will often play the piece at half-tempo or below to double check that I have internalized the music correctly. As Chef Hemphill said, "The discipline required for slow, careful practice is a major commitment."

5. With the ever-present danger of repetitive motion ailments and injuries, it is crucial that one takes brief breaks from playing to relax a bit during all practice sessions. Stretching and mild flexing motions, away from the instrument and without anything in the hands, can relax the shoulders, arms, wrists, hands, and fingers. The break is also important to the mind, as it is critical to be refreshed and alert mentally if the practice session is to provide significant results. Chef Hemphill says, "With a goal-driven orientation, time management is also important to the practice routine." Frequent breaks provide time to reflect on the past session and adjust strategies accordingly.

6. Repetition is an essential part of any practice session, especially when learning new material. Divide the music into short phrases, and practice each phrase many times consecutively. Using a metronome, set a tempo at which you can play a phrase easily and without mistakes. Play it several times at this tempo and then move the metronome up in tempo slightly. Continue the process until the desired tempo has been reached, then move on to the next section.

Once all the sections can be played at the desired tempo, set the metronome to a slower tempo and string the phrases together into larger sections. Play the combined larger sections multiple times, until they can be played comfortably, without mistakes, and then slowly increase the metronome again.

Playing with a metronome, drum machine, or computer sequencer is great in developing a clock-steady pulse, but be sure to spend some of your practice time performing without the metronome, too. This ensures that you have internalized the rhythm correctly to the pulse in your mind, and that you are not solely relying on the metronome to provide you with a sense of pulse.

7. The musician not only strives for accurate muscle memory ("auto-pilot" mode), but should also strive for awareness on many different levels. These levels include physical awareness of activity, aural awareness, visual awareness, and the awareness of sensation or feeling. Through controlled repetition, one can focus upon the feel of the activity and the accompanying motion involved. Without the help of a mirror or other visual aid, this tactile sensory development is important.

Developing this feeling of what it is like to perform effortlessly is critical, but the mind needs to be engaged and alert in the process of building the musical coordination and physiological movements as they are "programmed" into the muscles. Try repeating a phrase for three or four minutes without pause instead of playing it a certain number of times (which would require the brain to count and be distracted from the levels of awareness). Use a kitchen timer or alarm to count the minutes so you can focus your attention exclusively on the many levels of "feeling" the movement is producing.

8. Practice difficult passages above the designated tempo. This will allow you to relax and play expressively during performance. You can extract a difficult passage, adjusting it slightly, if necessary, to make a technical exercise where the technical challenge is purposefully increased (e.g., repeat challenging parts, add ornamentation, etc.). This will serve to make the original passage seem easier and will undoubtedly expand your technical facility.

9. Practice is a life-long process, so demand that when you practice you always play musically. Develop a "singing style," with artistic qualities, on all the instruments to help convey your ideas and emotions to the audience. Communication starts in the practice room. Carefully listen back to recordings of your practice sessions and compare them to what you "think" you are saying musically.

10. Repeat this recipe daily, because practice does not make perfect. *Perfect practice makes perfect.*

This practice recipe is based on a handout by Dr. Steve Hemphill, Percussion Professor at Northern Arizona University. ➤●

Improving Time Feel

Rod Morgenstein

In today's world of music and drumming, a great deal of emphasis is focused on pushing the "technique" envelope, striving for the highest levels of hand/foot independence, or attempting to enter the record books with the fastest hands and feet. While these are noble pursuits, it is important to not lose focus on what is, perhaps, one of *the* most important, and in-demand, drumming skills: the ability to count off a song and play with a consistent time feel throughout the song's entirety. All music, regardless of style, requires a drummer to have a strong inner clock, which will help lock in every musician while keeping the groove consistent and strong. Our goal is to improve our inner clock, which will strengthen our time feel and have musicians breaking down our doors to jam with us!

INGREDIENTS:
Drumsticks
Drum pad
Drumset
Metronome or metronomic device (e.g., a drum machine)
Headphones (in order to hear the metronome when playing the drumset)
Any drumset book that includes basic drum grooves (e.g., *The Drumset Musician*)

SERVES:
Beginners and up.

The metronome is the key component in helping us achieve an improved time feel. Sitting at the drum pad, set the metronome to quarter note =160 bpm and play alternating quarter notes, trying to match your strokes perfectly with the click. Do this for at least one minute. (Count in 4/4 time. If you are using a Dr. Beat rhythm machine or similar device, program it for 4/4 time.)

Now cut the number of bpms in half; 160 bpm divided by two = 80 bpm. Continue to think of 160 bpm as the quarter-note pulse. Now, the new 80 bpm clicks are half notes. Silently, try to hear quarter notes in your head. At 80 bpm, the half notes are sounding on beats 1 and 3. So, you must fill in the quarter notes, in your head, on beats 2 and 4. This "silent" technique is commonly referred to as "subdividing the measure." Subdividing the measure is one of the key elements in improving one's inner clock, which will, ultimately, vastly improve a drummer's time feel.

Now, play alternating half notes, trying to match your strokes perfectly with the click. This exercise will be somewhat more of a challenge than the previous one because, as the length of time between clicks increases, so does the difficulty in matching your strokes with the click. Do this for at least one minute.

Increase the challenge by, once again, cutting the number of clicks in half; 80 bpm divided by two = 40 bpm. As before, continue to think of 160 bpm as the quarter-note pulse. And so, the new 40 bpm clicks are whole notes. At 40 bpm, the whole notes are sounding on beat 1. Silently, sub-divide quarter notes on beats 2, 3, and 4.

Now, play alternating whole notes, matching your stroke exactly with the click. Do this for at least one minute.

Moving to the drumset, reset the metronome to 160 bpm, put on your headphones, open up your drumset book to a page of basic eighth-note grooves, and play each beat for at least one minute. Do not switch riding surfaces in the middle of a particular beat.

In striving for consistency, it is also very important to be aware of how your body is moving: hands, arms, torso. Try to lock in with the metronome. If you occasionally do not hear a click, it means that you are playing so perfectly in time with it that you actually "buried the click"!

As we did earlier on the drum pad, cut the number of clicks in half; 160 bpm divided by two = 80 bpm. Remember, the new 80 bpm clicks are half notes. It is your job to subdivide the measure. The half note clicks are sounding on beats 1 and 3, so you must fill in the quarter notes, in your head, on beats 2 and 4. Play each of the basic eighth note grooves for at least one minute.

For the ultimate drumset timing challenge, cut the number of clicks in half; from 80 bpm to 40 bpm. With the click at 40 bpm being a whole note (you already know that by now!), sub-divide the measure, hearing quarter notes on beats 2, 3, and 4. Play through the eighth-note grooves, focusing all your energy on locking in with the whole-note metronomic pulse.

Build on these basic grooves (and eventually more syncopated grooves) by playing assorted drum fills. Always think musically. For instance, play the beat for three measures and follow it with a one-measure fill. Or play the beat for two measures, followed by a two-measure fill.

Make practicing with a metronomic device an integral part of your practice routine. It will not cause you to play stiff or machine-like. Rather, it will improve your inner clock by leaps and bounds and vastly improve your time feel and overall drumming consistency. ➤

A Tasty Alternative for the Light Practice Schedule

Valerie Dee Naranjo

It takes a balanced diet of careful practice (and making music with others!) to build and maintain great musicianship. The following recipe is *not* meant to replace that kind of diet. This is a light meal to prepare daily when you are on the road, on vacation immediately before a recital, visiting family, or even doing lots of gigs that are not specifically related to your current practice goals—any time that you wish to grow, yet know that your practice time is limited. (Of course, you need to be lucky enough to have access to a couple of hours and instruments.)

INGREDIENTS:
Determination
More focus than normal
Patience
A good sense of humor
1 reliable recording device
1 stopwatch
1 chart (paper, pencil, straight edge ruler)
Instruments
Sticks and/or mallets

SERVES:
Those who need to keep musically fit in situations that don't include very much practice time.

PERSONNEL:
1 strict, yet reasonable, master chef (you)
1 enthusiastic, confident, and obedient sous chef (also you)

This style of cooking requires that both chefs work carefully with uncompromising determination. In general, it is easy to waste practice energy. Often the majority of our distractions come from our own mind. (What time is that sound check on Tuesday? Why did she say that about me?) You need to work to remove these distractions. Remove phones and e-mail access from this power-cooking session! Another primary life practice in general is to allow yourself the time and place to clear you mind, answer that call, say the "I'm sorrys" that you need to, feed your dog, etc.—anything that clouds your mind with "unfinished business."

The Chart

The chart represents what you have decided to accomplish in a set time frame (say, one week). List your activities down the left side of a standard sheet of paper, starting with the general practice time in total, and the dates across the top from left to right. You will use two columns per day: one for the amount of time that you wish to spend on each activity, another for what actually happens.

Now prioritize your activities into (1) most important (2) second most important. Determine how much time you have (no matter how limited) and divide that time accordingly. For example, I might have six important issues:

1. my open slap on djembe (for a recording session next week);

2. the climactic phrase of the next recital marimba solo (I had trouble with it during my last recital);

3. new charts for a percussion ensemble concert that I must read through and determine stickings etc. (for three weeks from now);

4. maintain the expression in the quick tempo of a gyil tune (for tomorrow's clinic);

5. my reading in bass clef (to improve my general skills);

6. brushing up on an old vibe solo (that I'd like to add to my repertoire).

With a few minutes over your morning tea you can determine, for example, that with two hours and 15 minutes of practice time you can assign 20 minutes each to three "second most important" issues and 25 minutes each to three "most important" issues. (Times will vary according to how familiar you are to an item, how difficult it is, etc. Make the adjustments by trial and error.) Write your time determinations in the left of the two columns for that day.

Now you (as the master chef) must obey the chart. Set your stopwatch. Make a fun game out of "seeing" what you can do in 20 minutes. Remember even the most tedious music is, by its nature, fun! This is, however, probably not the time to impress yourself by playing through the things that you do well. You *must* maintain confidence in your strong points and concentrate on strengthening your weak points. If it is appropriate, use the final minutes of your time to record yourself, then listen to the results later (by yourself on the train ride home from the day's final gig, for example.) When the stopwatch announces the end of your time limit for that segment of practice, reset it and move on.

Don't be hard on yourself if you fall short of your short-term goal. Tomorrow you can try again. Musicianship is a work in progress. Give yourself a special reward for your work. (If you are on vacation, it might be good to do this session early, if possible, so that you can then enjoy a day of sightseeing.)

Inevitably, at first and at other times, you will run off track (e.g., lose your keys, become absorbed in one thing only). Don't worry. The repetition of these efforts, when practice time is limited, will serve up a meal that might surprise you! ➟

Junk Food

Mark Nauseef

One of the most enjoyable and challenging aspects of being an improvising percussionist is the idea of performing on an instrument of which you have very little knowledge or experience. This happens because, although percussionists may be heavily trained in the percussive arts from an early age and/or have played drums their entire life, they can easily be thrilled by an unusual sound and then take time to develop a technique for making music with the object producing that sound. This situation happens to many percussionists, more than any other instrumentalists, as most percussionists are always searching for new sounds to add to their vocabulary.

INGREDIENTS:
Anything and everything, including the kitchen sink
Imagination

SERVES:
All creative percussionists.

New sounds are more often than not found in locations other than musical instrument shops. The "instruments" that produce these new sounds may be "found objects" such as kitchen utensils—the obvious being pots and pans, which ironically is how many percussionists started playing as children, but also electric mixers and egg slicers—containers made of metal, plastic, wood, and glass, as well as anything else that speaks to the explorer. Making wind chimes from handfuls of metal knives, forks, and spoons, or just throwing them all into a large empty metal container or galvanized garbage can could be your new instrument.

Find the sounds within the object, develop a technique to access those sounds, and create something with them. Although the kitchen is very rich in resources for new sounds, any place may be rewarding when searching for new instruments: old hubcaps from the garage, discarded metal lamp shades, or that protective screen/grate from a broken fan that may be hiding in the basement or attic. Outside the house there are many possibilities, as nature gives us much great-sounding wood, stone, pods filled with seeds, dried leaves, and so on.

Good-sounding found objects can be discovered everywhere, and the keys to discovery are looking, listening, and imagination. Toys are another source of sound. It's fun to tear open a toy to find out what is making that weird sound inside, then finding ways of manipulating and possibly extending that sound through modification of the object, and eventually adding it to a developing instrument made up of many sounds from individual instruments of choice. These instruments can be made from anything in the universe (or elsewhere) that produces a sound.

Extended techniques are always being created to extract sound from unlikely places and/or to modify sounds from likely sources. As well as striking with both hands and all fingers, the possibilities could include sticks, chains, mallets and beaters of all sizes and materials such as wood, metal, plastic, rubber, yarn, etc. As with kitchen sounds, good toy sounds may be electronic (battery operated) or acoustic, and techniques could include squeezing, shaking, scraping, spinning, pulling, winding, bowing, rubbing, and kicking.

As found objects and toys will eventually deteriorate and at some point be discarded, they may both be included in the third and most all-inclusive of categories of newly discovered instruments: "junk." Junk instruments are rubbish. Tons of rubbish are thrown out every day—discarded heaps for most people, a musical goldmine full of possibilities and joy for the improvising percussionist. The choice is large for great sound-producing objects, especially if you are looking for things to hit. Although there are possibilities for discovery by wind and string players, the most fortunate tend to be percussionists. All objects already mentioned, such as kitchen items and toys, will eventually find their way to the dump. You can find pipes, large sections of air ducts, grills, gratings. and rejected electronic equipment such as electric motors, broken cassette recorder/players and malfunctioning CD players.

Such composers as John Cage, John Bergamo, and Lou Harrison have written for automobile brake drums, and they are used in many classic pieces of percussion ensemble music. Cage wrote for tin cans, electric buzzers, radios (could be discarded/junk); Harrison wrote for oxygen tanks struck with baseball bats, rice bowls, large boxes; Harry Partch built instruments of liquor and wine bottles, airplane gas tanks, shell casings; and, of course, the master of junk mayhem, Spike Jones, used duck calls, guns, and whoopee cushions. Barbara Benary's instruments, which she built for her gamelan ensemble, Gamelan Son of Lion, included hubcaps used as gongs and resonators made of coffee cans.

In recent years, junk has gained more mainstream exposure through the popular performances of groups such as Stomp, who exclusively use junk and found objects, Blue Man Group, who use self-built instruments made of PVC piping, and Don "The Junk Man" Knaack, who composed and performed the music for Twyla Tharp's dance piece "Surfer at the River Styx" entirely on junk instruments.

In the world of "free improvised music," musicians often take an approach of accepting the junk completely as the piece of junk that it is as opposed to having a preconceived idea as to how it might be used, as in the case of substituting a hubcap for a gong in an American gamelan ensemble. British improvisers such as Tony Oxley, Frank Perry, and Paul Lytton have explored the possibilities of using found objects and junk in free improvised music.

One of the most fascinating of the free improvisers promoting junk usage in free improvised music is Jamie Muir, a truly original musician who relishes rubbish and would prefer not to "transmute rubbish" but "approach the rubbish with a total respect for its nature as rubbish." Here are a few of Muir's thoughts on the subject of rubbish: "I much prefer junk shops to antique shops. There's nothing to find in an antique shop—it's all been found already—whereas in a junk shop it's only been collected. But a rubbish dump has been neither found nor collected—in fact it's been completely rejected—and that is the undiscovered/unidentified/unclaimed/unexplored territory—the future if only you could see it."

He goes on to say, "Instead of transmuting rubbish into a music with a heavily qualitative bias...leave behind the biases and structures of selectivity (which is an enormous task), the "found" attitudes you inherit, and approach the rubbish with a total respect for its nature as rubbish—the undiscovered/unidentified/unclaimed—transmuting the nature into the performing dimension. The way to discover the undiscovered in performing terms is to immediately reject all situations as you identify them (the cloud of unknowing), which is to give music a future." (From a 1972 issue of *Microphone* magazine. These statements were reprinted in the book *Improvisation: Its Nature and Practice In Music* by Derek Bailey, first published in 1980.)

In another extract from the *Microphone* article, Muir says, "Improvising percussionists are primarily concerned with effecting alchemical changes over rubbish. The changes can be directed towards objective ends—beauty/purity/music—or subjective ends—an essentially organic interest in the process of change/transmutation itself." (From "Derek Bailey and the Story of Free Improvisation" by Ben Watson, 2004.)

One of my most memorable experiences with junk was when I was a member of Edward Vesala's Sound And Fury. My role as a percussionist in that band had me mostly hitting, kicking, Superballing, scraping, and chain whipping as well as leaping against a large double-basin steel sink that Vesala, Jimi Sumen, and other Sound And Fury members had salvaged from a dump in Helsinki. Sumen had also fixed guitar machine heads to the basin edge so that strings could be stretched across the sink, which gave me further possibilities to pluck, snap, pull, slide on, and detune strings. Not easy to transport, but a wonderful instrument. Another great junk experience was playing the part for a 747 jet engine cowling in live performances of John Bergamo's "On The Edge"—throwing pool balls around the gutter of the cowling, bowing the edge, Superballing, using barbeque skewers.

One positive bi-product of playing junk is that you can more easily develop your own unique technique and sound, as your instrument will be unlike any other—a healthy alternative to chasing the latest snare drum buying fashion or the cymbal setups of popular drummers. Found objects, toys, and junk are three general areas to be explored as first instruments as opposed to ornamental sounds—although it's hard to imagine being a virtuoso whoopee cushionist! ➤●

Analytical Listening

Terry O'Mahoney

Recording and analyzing one's own performance is the best way to assess progress and identify musical problems. The goal of this recipe is to teach students how to be more self aware, be objective about their performance, identify musical challenges, and become more efficient in their practice regimens.

INGREDIENTS:
Sticks/mallet/brushes
Recording device (tape recorder, digital recorder, video recorder, metronome, play-along tracks)
Any instrument

SERVES:
Any musician.

I cannot recall doing it more than a few times growing up. When I finally did it, the experience was quite shocking, yet revealing. It can be one of the most devastating things to do in your musical life. "It" is hearing your own performance on tape, CD, or video. One of my students describes the experience as "brutal," and indeed it is—brutally honest.

Young musicians often do not have an accurate idea of what they *really* sound like. They listen to themselves practice but have no objective, concrete way of assessing their own musical progress. Anyone aspiring to musical heights *must* be able to be self critical, and recording a practice session, rehearsal, or performance is the best way to do that. I often tell my students, "I hear you an hour every week, but *you* hear yourself the rest of the week. Who do you think is going to have the most time to analyze and decide what and how to practice?"

Listening to yourself perform is one of the most egotistically difficult things to do, but it is also the best way to get better. I am often surprised by how reticent students are to listen to their own playing. I attribute this to everyone's natural hesitancy to "face the truth." My belief in this method began when a student was working on improvisation and I was offering comments on his time feel, dynamic contrast, cohesiveness, etc., and he was skeptical of some of my observations. I thought, "If only he could hear what I'm hearing, it would be perfectly clear."

So, in that moment of enlightenment, I pulled out a tape recorder and recorded the rest of the lesson. When I played it back for him, he immediately recognized many (if not all) of the things I was saying. He couldn't argue with what his own ears were telling him.

Students often think recording themselves is inherently negative. It's not. It is a completely objective way of assessing a performance. Often students find they do some things well, which is reassuring. The trick is to continue to do what they do well and isolate what needs refining.

Many students listen to recordings for inspiration and ideas, which is great. The problem arises when they forget that the people they are hearing on record were once at the same place they are now—struggling to get better. They did not hear Jack DeJohnette when he was working on his snare drum comping, or Horacio Hernandez when he was developing his mambo groove.

Another common practice is to play along with records in order to achieve the proper feel for music, and this can be a very valuable learning tool. Often, however, students are not able to separate the performance on the record from themselves. Basically, they give themselves too much credit for sounding exactly like the record, when if fact they are not close to achieving the proper feel and spirit of the recording.

I record myself as much as possible. I know I have learned the most about my own playing in recording studios, where I played something and immediately heard it back to check for errors. As I was listening back to what I just played, I would think, "Yes, that part was okay," "Whoa, that fill didn't work there," or "I need to change how I'm doing that section." It is basically a form of editing. These decisions are all aspects of performing that are easy to make in hindsight but are difficult to make "in the moment" of music-making. Students often have trouble with this facet of performance because they are so busy making the music (from a technical standpoint) that they cannot hear what they are doing objectively. They also often miss "the big picture." For example, they may sound fine by themselves, but they aren't together with the other members of the ensemble.

I often videotape students in order to show them how they *move* as well as sound. They are often surprised by how much energy and motion they waste when playing. When discussing hand position, posture, stick height, angle of attack, or a number of other visually notable aspects of performance, video is invaluable. Just like using a mirror in the practice room, the video clearly delineates any technical flaws. Once students grow accustomed to seeing themselves on video, they appreciate its benefits.

Recording devices today are so easy to use and relatively inexpensive. I frequently use a play-along track (played through overhead stereo speakers) and record the student separately on a digital recorder. Using this method, students are able to hear the recording *and* their performance and check for how well they are synchronizing with the record.

Although hearing themselves is important, the analysis of that recording is the most important aspect of the process. Students need to develop self-analysis skills. When playing a groove or rhythmic pattern and it is uneven, they need to be deciphering "why" it is not right. For example, they may have a tendency to drag quarter-note triplets, or have difficulty changing subdivisions (particularly triplets to sixteenths and back). If they can identify their own tendencies, they can focus on these things immediately and not mindlessly run over passages not knowing what's wrong or how to fix it.

I routinely videotape students' juries (performance exams). At the lesson immediately following the exam, I play the tape for them, we go over each comment I made on their evaluation sheet, and I ask them to offer their observations as the tape is rolling. They often focus on things I am not concerned with (their facial expressions), but that is to be expected. What they do see is their performance from my perspective, and often admit that many (if not all) of the suggestions I made in their lessons were valid.

While reviewing the recording, I simultaneously dissect their performance and ask a series of questions:

1. Overall observations about the recording: good, bad, okay, excellent.

2. How was the time feel?

3. Balance: Do all parts of the drumset sound cohesive or is one part sticking out?

4. Dynamic control/contrast: was it monodynamic or did it have a shape?

5. When improvising, was the soloing interesting to the listener, was it technically solid, was it stylistically correct/appropriate?

6. If using a play-along track, how well did the student sync with the recording?

7. Were the fills at the right place and stylistically suitable?

8. If using brushes, was the sound smooth and consistent or choppy and disjunct?

9. What was the quality of sound produced? Was it is harsh (perhaps from striking the cymbals too hard) or fluid (when just the right touch is used)?

10. Was the overall performance musical?

This list is not definitive but is a good start on the road to self-awareness. Teaching students to assess themselves is the first step to their musical independence. I know it has been an invaluable part of my teaching for years.

From a teacher's perspective, there is one other advantage to recording students' performances. Particularly when students perform for a grade (e.g., in an academic setting), a recording of their performance is empirical evidence of their achievement. Without the recording, students (or in some cases a parent) could later argue that "I really played that well" or "I thought I deserved a higher grade." Since I've started recording students playing exams, not a single student has challenged his or her grade. ➡

A Deeper Groove

Jim Payne

Questions such as "How do I get a deeper pocket, a more organic feel, a fatter groove, a more relaxed groove, a more laid-back groove" are often treated as mysteries or even as unteachable. Common answers include: You either have it or you don't; You just feel it; You're born with it; It's in your blood; and so on.

I'd like to offer some ideas that have worked for me in dealing with these questions.

INGREDIENTS:
One person, willing and able.
Drumset or hand percussion instrument (congas, timbales etc.).
Simple sequencer or computer recording software. (These last items are optional.)

SERVES:
Percussion players in general and drumset players in particular—all levels.

Why is it that when we play a simple rock-type beat, everybody says, "Okay, alright," but when Steve Gadd plays the exact same beat, everybody says, "Yeah! That's what we want! Wow! Incredible!"?

Obviously it has something to do with the *way* he plays it, the sound quality and, most important, the *feel*. And when you watch Steve play, he has a certain body motion—a certain rocking motion—and you also get the feeling that he's totally glued to the seat. Nothing's gonna move him.

Let's see if we can get a little closer to what's going on here. Steady, relaxed groove making, that's for sure, and that's what we're after.

First, let's talk about posture. I like to emulate Tony Williams in this respect. Basically, sit up straight. Arms naturally at the sides. Sit high enough so the thighs are angled down and the leg muscles are not cramped. I noticed that Elvin Jones sat higher in his later years to alleviate leg problems he was having. The taller the body frame, the higher the seat. If you play the ride cymbal a lot, set it up close enough so it isn't a strain to reach it. Otherwise just use common sense to arrange the pieces of the kit to make it easy for your arms and legs.

Better posture is the first step in eliminating tension, which I think we all suffer from—tension in the spine, the neck, the shoulders, etc. When I was learning to play in a big band at the Jazzmobile program in Harlem, Frank Foster, the famous tenor player who played with Elvin after Coltrane passed away and who led the Count Basie Orchestra for many years, came over to me after a tune and opened up his closed fist. "You've gotta open up your a**hole," he said. After being somewhat shocked, I realized what he was talking about. I played down the chart and didn't make many mistakes, but my tension was coming out in my playing and affecting the feel, making it stiff and nervous. And tension starts down there, at the lowest point, and then works its way upward. If you can relax at the bottom, you have a chance to avoid tension all the way up the spine, into the neck, shoulders, etc.

Yoga and Tai Chi can also mellow out the body, decrease tension, and cure some of those sore muscles. Tony Williams was into Tai Chi. After all, the Chi or life force is what we're using to get the job done. Any awareness and control of that has to be good.

Mind relaxation and focus are also important—again, Yoga and Tai Chi, and also meditation and chanting—something that calms the mind so its relentless spinning and grabbing of your attention doesn't take up all your time. The mind is an amazing machine that loves to work all the time, but what it chooses to work on may not be what *you* want to work on. It has to be tamed and controlled. It can be thinking about dinner when you want to be thinking about—or better yet, feeling—the groove.

Sit down like you mean it. Another image I've found useful is to imagine yourself a lineman (or linewoman) in the NFL—at least 300 lbs. Imagine that you're this person when you sit down at the drumset. When I see Bernard Purdie or Clyde Stubblefield sit at the set, I think of this—not that they weigh that much, of course! But the idea is that you're an immovable object, like a mountain. You're solid, and nothing (including the bass player) is going to move you.

Jabo Starks, one of the principal James Brown drummers, once told me, "The other guys can go and do their thing. When they get through, they'll come back and find me right here just like I was in the beginning, keeping that same groove."

Another indication of whether you're really relaxed is if your tongue is relaxed. The tongue, some say, is one of the centers of creativity. It's relaxed if the tip is touching the front of the palette where it meets the back of the front teeth, with the teeth just lightly touching. Also, no jaw clenching, something I'm unfortunately really good at.

Now we're set up and relaxed. This is where the fun begins.

I'm sure you've noticed what I call the "body motion" of different drummers. Some, like Bernard Purdie, have a left leg pump: bouncing on the ball of the foot as that foot sits on the closed hi-hat. Ringo sways his head back and forth. Other drummers have other motions. I'm not recommending any of these, but just mentioning that we already use our bodies to get ourselves into the groove, whether it's conscious or not.

If we're sitting at the drumset or at the congas, and we're sitting like a mountain, very relaxed, not playing, we should feel a body motion, a back-and-forth motion from the butt to the head. This is the natural rhythm of the body. I'm not talking about the heartbeat. I have done some research on that, too, but I find that this natural body motion is more useful. For now we'll just go with whatever tempo is happening naturally. Just practice feeling that pulse.

Breathe normally. Don't worry about when you take each breath. Just make sure you're not holding your breath.

Music, especially the rhythm of music, and especially the rhythm of the drums, reflects the rhythm of nature, the world, the universe. Elvin Jones said he used to try to capture the rhythm of a thunderstorm or the rhythm of the wind or the rhythm of a river or a waterfall.

The pulse of drumming is so universal and so primordial, it seems as if it's always been and will always be. This is the pulse we are generating. We're expressing *our* pulse, which is really an example of the pulse of nature or the pulse of the universe.

So, how to get better at it without ignoring it and just playing from our minds or expressing our tension?

1. Go through the relaxation process as described above, consciously relaxing the various parts of the body—spine, shoulders, tongue, and jaw. Feel the pulse of your body motion.

2. Now play the world's simplest (and probably most popular) beat: boom-bap-boom-bap, (with eighths on the closed hi-hat). Conga players can play a simple *tumbao*. Feel the pulse as you play. You have to play something incredibly simple to be able to use part of your concentration to feel this pulse. Don't add any fills or complicate the beat with frills.

While feeling the pulse, using that as the tempo and coordinating the beat with this tempo, play a four-bar phrase, but stop on the downbeat of the fourth bar, and for the rest of the fourth bar, don't play, just feel that back-and-forth pulse. Play the next four bars the same way, stopping to feel the pulse in the fourth bar.

This is the whole idea of this recipe. I'm not saying you can do this on the gig, but if you practice it, it will help the groove on the gig. It will deepen the groove and make it more laid back. If you know the material really well and you know what you're playing really well, you may be able to feel this pulse at the same time. And you may be able to *trust* this pulse and use it to deepen your groove.

If the song tempo is slightly different, don't worry; you can will the pulse to change tempo. It's not that hard. It pretty much happens automatically.

Another aid, courtesy of John Riley: Put together a simple program with your sequencer or computer. Program a metronome to click quarter notes for eight bars of a medium-slow tempo, about mm = 80. Then program a click+crash (so you can hear it easily) on the downbeat of the next bar. Then program *nothing* for four bars. Continue to program click+crash on the downbeat of the first bar, then nothing for four bars until you have a total of 32 bars. Then repeat the whole 32-bar pattern several times. The beginning eight bars of click will help you get back on track just in case you happen to get off (which you and I and everyone else will definitely do!).

While you're in that "no man's land" where the time is going on but you're hearing nothing, it will be like playing a gig. You're on your own. And you can check yourself by seeing if you can hit that downbeat every four bars.

I've found that the easiest way to hit it is to tune into the body motion and *trust it*! I hit more downbeats that way than by concentrating real hard, or by subdividing. This really works.

You can program this sequence with several different tempos and also increase the silence to eight bars if you want to, but I think serious work with a medium-slow tempo and four-bar silence will do the trick. ➤●

Teaching a Fast Learner

Al Payson

This recipe is for training bright students, who typically bore easily and want to move on to a new skill or task before the current one is sufficiently mastered.

INGREDIENTS:
Bright student
Selected task
Play-along CD appropriate for the task
Conversation
Educational concept called The Four Stages of Learning.
CD player
Conversation starters (questions requiring long answers).

SERVES:
All quick-witted percussionists at any level of proficiency (as well as string and keyboard players).

First, an explanation of the operation of one of the "ingredients," the educational concept, is in order. In it, the process of learning is divided into four stages, which are called:

1. Unconscious incompetence
2. Conscious incompetence
3. Conscious competence
4. Unconscious competence

The four stages can perhaps best be explained by using the example of a student learning a certain task, such as learning to play alternating flams:

1. Unconscious incompetence: The teacher plays some alternating flams at a moderate pace and says to the student, "This is what you're going to learn next." The student sees and hears the teacher play the alternating flams, but has no idea how they're executed.

2. Conscious incompetence: The teacher explains and demonstrates very slowly how the alternating flams are executed, and has the student perform the rudiment slowly. The student understands what is required, but cannot consistently perform the rudiment correctly.

3. Conscious competence: The student practices alternating flams until he can perform them correctly and on a fairly consistent basis, but only if he gives the task 100% concentration. As soon as he loses concentration, it falls apart.

4. Unconscious competence: The student practices the rudiment until he can perform it on "auto-pilot," and focus his attention elsewhere.

This concept of learning can be applied to almost any task, even learning to walk. An important objective is to have music students bring every task they are given up to stage four so their minds are free to focus on other issues, such as ensemble and musicality. Different teachers have different ways of explaining this final stage. Author/drummer Mike Lankford, in his memoir *Life in Double Time*, wrote "To think too much about what you're doing is to handicap yourself and sound musically wooden. The muscles must learn on their own, the body develops its own coordination, while your attention goes entirely to the overall effect you're producing."

It has been my experience that a common trait among bright students is that they go through stages two and three very quickly, then feel the task is completed and/or do not have the patience to repeat the task enough to get to stage four. Being mentally agile, they tend to become bored very quickly with repetition and want to move on to the challenge of a new task.

Once the ingredients required for this recipe are assembled and understood, we are ready for the next phase.

Preparation

1. Assign the bright student a task, such as a certain technique, and lead him or her through stages one, two, and three.
2. To minimize the boredom of the repetitions required to get to stage four, "mix in" having the student play along with a CD, particularly with tracks that are at least two to three minutes in length. Along with keeping the student mentally occupied, this has the added benefit of forcing him or her to play with a steady pulse.

Determining When the Recipe is "Done"

An easy way to determine if students have achieved stage four is to engage them in conversation while they play. Try doing the following right now: play alternating flams, just with your hands on your knees, and at the same time read aloud the rest of this paragraph. If you can do so without the slightest mistake in either the hands or the recitation, you are at stage four.

I usually initiate a conversation by asking the student questions that require lengthy answers. The question, "Do you like baseball?" is not very good for this situation, at least for older students, because they can just answer "yes" or "no." "What is your schedule for the rest of the day?" is much better. Most students seem to enjoy the challenge of this test and get a great deal of satisfaction in passing it. And in time they see the value of it.

Incidentally, there does not seem to be an age that is too young to apply this "recipe." Here is a quote of master teacher Shinichi Suzuki from his book *Nurtured by Love*:

> When the children have learned how to play "Twinkle, Twinkle, Little Star" variations easily and freely, I ask them to play them, and I say, "Now let's play a game. I want you to answer my questions while you go on playing. Answer in a loud voice, and don't stop playing." Then, in a loud voice, I call out, "How many legs have you?" They think this is loads of fun, and answer all together at the top of their voices, "Two." Now, if they can do this while playing correctly, it means that the skill has been properly inculcated and has become second nature. If among them there is a child for whom it is not yet second nature, he will be so intent on his playing that he does not reply. Or if he replies, he will stop playing. I ask many different questions and they answer while playing. Smiling sweetly, they have acquired the ability to play games with me while they go on playing the violin. Every single child, without fail, gets so he can do this.

I hope you enjoy using this recipe as much as I have.

How to Get Good

Jeff Queen

This recipe will help any players looking to improve their skills through consistent practice. I will outline the steps that I took in order to get better and use snare drumming as the main example. Even though snare drumming is used, this process can apply to any instrument or skill that one desires to improve upon.

INGREDIENTS:

Physical
1 metronome
1 mirror
1 pair of sticks
1 pad or drum

Mental
A never-ending supply of patience (you have it, really you do!)
Persistence
Dedication of the everyday variety
Passion
And why not throw in some more patience while we are at it?

Recommended Sides
1 chair
1 snare stand
1 music stand
Method book. Be honest with your abilities: If you are just starting out, get a beginner book; if you have been playing for a while, use an intermediate book; etc.
Private teacher

Optional Spices
Tape recorder (to listen to yourself)
Video recorder (to see yourself)
Solos—all difficulty levels

SERVES:
All players who desire to get better.

One of the most important things for this recipe to turn out correctly is the proper environment in which you choose to "cook." Your "kitchen" should be free from distractions, well lit, clean, and accessible. The more convenient and clean your ingredients are, the more apt you are to use them.

A little side note: When I was growing up, I would get five minutes in here and there—between TV shows, right after dinner, or before I left for school. Sometimes I would take a break from homework and play a roll for five minutes or just jam for a few. With this type of schedule, having all my practice materials easily accessible made these small bits of time very productive. (Now back to the recipe.)

Double check your inventory the first time you sit down; having to run to the store to pick up a missing ingredient will cut into your practice time. Also, when you first get going, you may have to "practice practicing." When I am not good at something, it is not a lot of fun to do it at first, and most anything can get in my way, giving me an excuse *not* to practice. Give yourself every reason *to* practice. It is hard enough to talk yourself into it, let alone if you don't have the right pair of sticks, the wrong space, no drum/pad, etc. Having all your ingredients set up at all times takes away from any excuse to not practice.

Other than sticks and a pad, the metronome is the next most important thing (kind of like real butter: You can cook without it or use a substitute, but it sure tastes better with the real thing!) If you don't have access to a metronome, you can play along with your favorite tune (and you know what to request for your next birthday/holiday). Realize that playing in tempo with correct rhythmic interpretation is a vital skill for any musician.

Got everything? Great, now we're cookin' with gas!

Getting better can be thought of as a multiple-course meal, and we need to "cook" a few different dishes in order to complete the whole meal.

Course 1: The Timing Appetizer
The first course is "timing skills." For the most part, this dish comes in two flavors: Duple (groups of two, four, etc.) and triple (groups of three, six, etc.). If you can master the subdivisions/permutations of sixteenth notes (there are fourteen of them) and triplets (there are six of them) you will have the skills needed to cook any other dish you would like. This is also why we should taste this dish first; it will whet our palate for everything else we are going to eat. Think about it: Everything can be broken down into groups of two, three, or four, so in order to play/cook anything else, we need to understand how to correctly interpret these rhythms.

Start with the sixteenth-note permutations; these are a little more accessible to most people (like pizza; everybody likes pizza). All the sixteenth-note permutations can be broken down into one-, two-, or three-note groupings. Once you have mastered those with your metronome, move on to the triplets. The triple permutations can be broken down into either one- or two-note groupings. Try playing four of each permutation in a row and counting the downbeat out loud as you do it. This will help you understand how each rhythm relates to the beat and develop a much stronger sense of pulse and time.

This applies to any instrument.

Be sure to add the patience ingredient to every dish. It takes a considerable amount of time to simply improve (let alone get good) at any skill. Be patient with yourself, go slow, and make sure to learn things the correct way. This will save you a lot of time (and allow you to keep gigs) as you progress to the next level of your playing or career.

Course 2: Two-Height Control Salad

The next course is "two-height control." This is where the mirror comes in handy, as it will allow you to see your heights as you play them (the video camera is great here, too!). You can use a standard "bucks" exercise (on one hand, play a bar of eighth notes, accents on the downbeats and taps on the upbeats) or "triplet bucks" (accent the first beat of a triplet and play taps/low notes for the second and third). Two-height control is imperative for playing flams or most any other rudiment.

This applies to any instrument, one way or another. You need to know how to play loud, soft, and anywhere in between.

Once you have "digested" the bucks, try adding in taps on the other hand to create either accented sixteenth notes or sextuplets. Look in the mirror and be sure that this "looks like it sounds." By this I mean that the loud notes are high and the soft notes are low. Imagine what this would "sound" like to a deaf person; by seeing a clear definition to the heights, a deaf person might be able to "hear" what it sounds like by the way it looks.

One more little bit of tastiness before we move on to the main course...

Course 3: Note Grouping Soup

This scrumptious little treat is called "note groupings." Realize that most everything you play can be broken down into different note groupings, usually one, two, three, or four notes on a hand at a time. If you can get good at playing single notes (eight on a hand), doubles (double beats), triples (triple beats), and quadruple beats (four notes on a hand), then you can pretty much play anything. Master this skill at multiple heights (play an accent followed by a double, triple, or quad), and then you are really in business!

This can relate directly to other percussion instruments but could also be thought of as four-mallet permutations, heel-toe patterns, or basic grooves on hand drums, basic coordination exercises/grooves on drumset, etc.

Course 4: The Main Dish

Now, on to the main course! I am going to roll (pun intended) diddles and flams into the same dish. The main point here is that you have worked on some basic skills (timing, two-height control, and note groupings), and it is time to apply that to the rest of the vocabulary (rudiments) that you will use when playing the drum.

Realize what each rudiment/skill uses from the first few "courses" we have talked about. Everything is going to use the timing skill, and in order to figure out what the rest of it is, try playing a given rudiment with one hand on your drum/pad and the other on your leg. What you will hear is a one-handed breakdown of the rudiment/skill you are working on.

What do you hear? Now would be a great time to use the tape recorder or video camera so you can play yourself back and maybe even write out the rhythm! Try playing a flam accent; you should hear one loud note and three soft notes. A paradiddle-diddle? One loud note and two soft notes, and so on. By having a solid foundation in the skills above, you can break down any pattern/rudiment/skill and work on the fundamental skills required to play it.

Try playing any diddle rudiment, flam rudiment, or hybrid and see what combination of notes/accents it is made of. If you have mastered and truly "digested" the first few courses, the main dish is going to taste amazing and sit very comfortably in your belly.

This relates to any instrument and should be thought of as the culmination of multiple skills used together. Break down one hand/limb on drumset, one set of tones on hand drums, just the inside or outside mallet, etc.

Ready for some dessert? Great! Now that I have covered the fundamental skills needed to play most anything on a snare drum, for dessert I will share how to go about practicing these skills.

The One-Hour "Get Better" Dessert
First, just like eating, you have to practice and play every day. There is no magic dust or pill that will make you better. You have to put the time in to get better, just like you have to eat in order to stay alive.

Below is a breakdown of practice time that I suggest each day. I know time is scarce for most of us, but if you can find an hour somewhere in your day to practice, you will notice a far greater progression of your abilities than if you practice inconsistently.

I.   5-minute Warm Up: Stretch your muscles, get loose, work on a few basics.

II. 20-minute rudiment breakdown: Go slow, *really* slow, with perfect heights. This could translate to scales, mallet permutations, arpeggios, etc.

III. 5 minutes of sight reading.

IV. 25 minutes on etudes, exercises, etc. that are part of your lesson (remember getting that private teacher?). When practicing these, take small bites at a time. One count or one measure at a time, be patient and *go slow*; you don't want to choke!

V.   5-minute "chop out": Play a roll for 5 minutes, do the same permutation for 5 minutes, accented sixteenth notes, double verticals from a third to a fifth, etc, to work your muscles so they build up stronger.

Best of luck with your cooking (and eating)! A steady diet of all of the courses above will improve your abilities, regardless of what level you are as a player. It is my experience that everyone can use a refresher course in the basics, and after doing so, are much more solid and comfortable in their playing.

Remember that finding a daily routine and, most of all, having fun is the bottom line. It may take a while to notice some improvement (maybe you are not playing every day?), but if you go slow, are patient, and practice every day, it won't be long before you "get good." ➔

Feeding Difficult Students

John Riley

Some students unquestioningly devour every suggestion and assignment. With others it's a more collaborative effort. A small percentage of students seem unable or unwilling to accept guidance. In this article we will discuss strategies for helping these difficult students.

INGREDIENTS:
Identifying student's aspirations
Expanding student's circle of comfort
Insisting on mastery

SERVES:
Private teachers, band directors.

We've all experienced joy of playing the music we love. Practicing our favorite music is simply easier than practicing repertoire because we *need* to be able to perform repertoire on a particular occasion. Students feel the same way. Because the financial rewards of a career in music are modest, I believe it is crucial that students and professionals alike are focused on playing the music they love because there the curiosity is greater, motivation is stronger, diligence is higher, and those attributes all lead to a higher rate of success. Additionally, that joy I mentioned earlier may be the only compensation one receives on a given day.

A teacher is a source of information and inspiration: mentor, psychologist, confessor, and judge. Most students are somewhat informed and seek out a teacher they believe can help them to play the music they are most interested in. Others just end up on your doorstep.

As a nine-year-old student, I didn't know what I needed but I did know what I wanted: to be able to play the rock beats I was hearing on the radio and on my 45 rpm records. My teacher, Tom Sicola—then a freshman at the Manhattan School of Music with Jim Petercsak and Steve Gadd—was willing to meet my needs, but only after I completed the assignments he thought I needed, like learning a particular rudiment, a reading exercise from Haskell Harr book 1, the bossa nova pattern, or the major scales on vibes. This "carrot and stick" approach worked very well for both of us. Through Tom's guidance those rock beats got easier, but I also came to appreciate the value in practicing reading, learning various styles and playing mallets. I stayed with him for six years.

I've found the same method very effective with difficult older students *if* I can get them to reveal their true musical aspirations. Once you know their dreams, give them material to help that area, then continually introduce concepts that are one or two steps outside their comfort zone but in a direction that will be obviously beneficial to them there and will broaden their musicianship.

Think of a student's comfort zone as a circle, and work to gradually expand the diameter of that circle. Don't confuse professional courtesy with friendship; we must give students what we deem best, even if they don't "like" us for being so stern with them. However, even when I've considered a student's aspirations totally unrealistic or impractical, I have not had any success forcing students to immediately abandon their circle of comfort. Empathetic coaxing is more successful than strong-arming.

Teachers in school settings have an obligation to provide competent players for the various ensembles. Difficult students often refuse to see the value in playing in the school ensembles. Stress to them that excelling in school ensembles has many benefits: mastering the skills required for these school ensembles will only broaden their musicianship; through playing in the school ensembles a wider range of student musicians, and possible employers, will become aware of them; earning a place in the most visible ensembles will provide opportunities to play and be heard off campus, at conventions and with guest artists who could provide assistance later in the professional world.

If students don't respond to your input, perhaps they don't respect your opinion or playing. What can you do? Play a recording for them of music that they cannot comprehend, then calmly explain how they can use those concepts in their own playing. If that doesn't work, as a last resort, play something yourself that "blows them away." Inspire them and earn their respect.

Have students assess their own strengths and weaknesses. Help prioritize the weaknesses and create a list of goals. The keys to good playing on the drumset or any instrument are prioritized below. Make the lessons constructive and be sure the students understand what is being asked of them and how each particular assignment will be beneficial.

Absolute Goal: musicianship and groove

Main components: technique, creativity

Building blocks: rhythmic precision, concentration, listening, dexterity, dynamic control, touch, coordination, reading, form, styles.

Take an interest in the student's perspective by periodically asking what new music the student has been exploring. Encourage students to practice and listen to music together. Playing music is not a competition but getting gigs is highly competitive; a little friendly rivalry among students can be very healthy. ➥

It's All About the Basics

Lisa Rogers

Just as a well-stocked kitchen is necessary for a chef to make a masterful dinner, the keyboard percussionist needs a well-stocked arsenal of techniques to present memorable performances. For a keyboard percussionist, time spent discovering and employing the basic elements of technique will improve accuracy and sound production. There are several basic ingredients the two-mallet keyboard percussionist should keep on hand to improve performance skills. If a two-mallet player emphasizes these elements when performing, he or she should notice increased accuracy, consistent sound production, and efficiency of motion.

INGREDIENTS:
Stance
Body position
Grip
Stroke
Stickings

SERVES:
Keyboard percussionists at all levels.

Stance
Try keeping feet almost shoulder width apart in order to move easily and fluidly from side to side with the instrument for better accuracy and sound production. Avoid taking too many steps as you move throughout the range of the instrument. Too many steps tend to shift your center of gravity and compromise accuracy.

Body Position
If your instrument is height adjustable, adjust it the same way you would adjust your snare stand. This will allow for maximum efficiency of body motion and, in turn, will help accuracy. If the instrument is not height adjustable, place blocks of wood underneath to raise the instrument slightly or build a wooden platform to stand on while playing if reaching the instrument is difficult.

If you are having trouble reading music, adjust the music stand. Don't move your body closer to or further away from the instrument, resulting in poor or uneven sound production.

Grip
Two-mallet grip is similar to matched snare drum grip; however, try to fit the mallets almost in the groove of each palm or slightly offside. This placement will allow the mallets and wrists to move in up-and-down motions efficiently so the mallets contact the bars accurately.

Every pair of mallets has an ideal balance point (where the mallets will rebound the most). Even though the bars of a mallet instrument don't rebound like the batter head of a snare drum, the balance of a mallet is extremely important for efficiency of motion and accuracy. Test the rebound capabilities of your mallets on a drum pad or snare drum. Position your fulcrum (thumb and first finger grip) at various points along the mallet. Then, drop with a weighted wrist motion and check the number of rebounds. When you find the ideal balance point, you have also found where your fulcrum should be placed on the mallet.

Stroke

Try thinking about one stroke per wrist motion. As you strike a bar, follow through and return to the starting point in preparation for striking the next bar. Don't strike the bar, stop, and lift again as preparation for the next stroke. This results in more effort with two motions and possible loss of accuracy.

Stickings

Fluidity of sound and accuracy on a keyboard instrument is also dependent on the stickings chosen by the performer. Most of the time, strict alternation of mallets provides a sense of flow and smoothness to the sound production. Accuracy is improved as well. However, there may be times when double stickings need to be employed to avoid leaps or "crossing" of mallets, which again should improve accuracy and sound production. Marking the stickings on a piece of music can be very valuable in enhancing motion memory and thus repeated accuracy.

The Musical Meal

Utilizing and understanding the basic ingredients and techniques needed for an impeccable meal or a superior performance will always prove successful to whoever is served. Whether an aspiring cook or master chef or beginning or advanced keyboard percussionist, it's all about the "basics"!

Recipe for an Orchestral Percussion Audition

Michael Rosen

Everyone knows the recipe for getting an orchestral job: play the best. But how does one put together the ingredients in the right proportions so that you can actually serve yourself "well done" at the audition? What can you expect at an audition? It's not enough to just know the excerpts flawlessly—although that is the ingredient basic to all successful auditions. Here is a recipe for success that, if followed diligently, will help you make a dish that you will be proud to serve to any audition committee.

INGREDIENTS:
A large measure of raw talent
Hours of practice marinated in patience until perfect
Freshly ground motivation
Dash of common sense
A few pinches of courage
A set of mallets to suit the situation

SERVES:
Everyone who is determined.

In addition to specific excerpts that are asked for at an audition, the audition committee will often ask for rolls at various dynamic levels (snare drum, tambourine, triangle, bass drum); a solo composition of the auditioner's choice (marimba or xylophone); and, in one case I know of, improvisation on tambourine. Expect to be asked to sight-read on every instrument.

At many auditions one is asked to play cymbal crashes at various dynamic levels. In some cases the orchestra will tell you which edition or which book a given excerpt can be found, in which case, use that version. Often they will insist you read from the provided edition that sometimes is furnished beforehand to qualified applicants. However, it is always in your best interest to practice from the original part so as to avoid errors that seem to appear in reprints of excerpts.

Auditioners are sometimes requested to bring their own instruments and sometimes their own music, but usually instruments and music are provided. More often the specific instruments provided are listed, and in some cases the dimensions of the instruments are furnished. By all means take instruments with you if you wish, but avoid having to set up very much at an audition (especially in the first round) because the committee does not want to waste time waiting for you. If you delay too long before you begin, they might become impatient and think less of your professionalism.

In some cases it is better to play the instruments provided because the audition committee is used to them and can better compare you to the other players. Do, by all means, raise the snare drum to a good level for you, but it is probably not a good idea to put blocks under the xylophone, which will take too much time. Practice playing mallet instruments set at various heights. When you get the job, you can make any adjustments you want.

More often than not, you are given a place to warm up, but it may be a large room where other auditioners are also waiting. Seldom will you be given a private room in which to warm up, and even less often will the instruments you are given be the same or even similar to the ones at the actual audition. It is a good idea to bring a practice pad with you on which to warm up. I suggest you have a 15-minute warm-up regimen that gets you focused and ready to play.

Do not feel intimidated by the other people at the audition and don't let their negative energy affect you; stay above it! I suggest you bring a Walkman or iPod with earphones so you can stay focused. Listen to whatever music makes you feel comfortable and reduces your stress level. I prefer Chopin "Nocturnes" because they have a calming effect, but choose whatever suits you. In any case, do not listen to the other auditioners play. We have a tendency to compare ourselves to others when we hear them, and that can have a negative effect on your performance. Let the judges do the comparisons; you just play your best!

Be prepared to play cold if necessary. You can practice this well before the audition by starting practice sessions playing the most difficult excerpts without warming up. Once you have mastered this, have a friend listen to you for this first rendition to create an audition atmosphere to help overcome nervousness. After you have mastered all the excerpts for an audition, practice on different instruments, in different rooms (try to get into a large auditorium to play on stage by yourself) and in front of friends (strangers would be even better). Ask friends to listen to you play a mock audition. The goal is to create an audition atmosphere so that you are ready for anything that might happen.

Seldom, if ever, will you be asked to play every excerpt on a given list, but you *must* be prepared with every one just in case. In addition, be sure to know the entire part on the audition—not just the few measures that we all know are the most difficult or the most likely to be asked. Auditions have been won or lost because a person was asked to play what they thought was the easy part of a composition that they didn't expect. In most cases a list is sent out to those who have been invited to play. More often than not, one is not asked to play the composition of choice, even though it may have been asked for on the list. More auditions are demanding drumset ability, so it is a good idea to have a good sense of basic styles of music on the drumset. In 1997 the Chicago Symphony asked players to choose one from a list of eight solo pieces to be played on marimba. If you audition for the Bogota Symphony in Columbia, be prepared to play traditional Columbia rhythms on tombora, cuchara, maracas, guiro, and congas!

The ability to play timpani seems to be more important at percussion auditions these days, even if the job is not advertised as a timpani job. Being able to play the essential timpani excerpts is very important, so be sure to work on them also. In the case of an opening for percussion/assistant timpani, you must go into the audition as though you were taking two complete auditions and study both repertoire lists.

Simply being able to play the excerpts note-perfect is not enough. One must know the context in which each belongs, correct tempi (playing too fast is a sure indication of an inexperienced player), and style. Play with a sense of the style that suits the music. Play with connection to the music, not just a string of cold, unconnected notes. Sing the part as you play and know how it fits into the context of the music. Try to bring something special to each excerpt. It could be special care to a dynamic, or arriving at a particularly important spot that emphasizes the phrasing, or perhaps special mallets. Learn the excerpts and be able to play them note-perfect and you could be well on your way to a job in a professional orchestra. However, there are more excerpts and no one knows what will be asked at the next audition.

Often a conductor will ask you to play an excerpt without his conducting you. Just as often he will conduct. The former is to test your experience and knowledge of the music, and the latter is to see how well you follow a conductor. Be prepared for both situations. In the finals, a conductor might ask you to change the way you play something simply to see how you react to criticism and how well you can adapt. Sometimes the position you are auditioning for is to replace a specific instrument in the percussion section, such as a cymbal player, mallet specialist, or snare drummer. Find out beforehand what the position is and practice that instrument with more diligence.

Because of the large number of applicants for each opening (250 or more!) it has become common for orchestras to have interested people send in tapes or have a preliminary audition. The conductor is usually not present at this segment of the audition process and depends on the audition committee to choose those best prepared to go on to the main audition where the conductor is present.

When you send in your application, the personnel manager will ask for your credentials, letters of recommendation, and perhaps a tape of specific excerpts. It is of *utmost* importance for you to realize that in the process of getting the job, this is probably the most important step. If you do not make a good first impression you won't even get a chance to play in person. It is absolutely essential that you make a first-rate professional tape. Do not borrow your cousin's cassette recorder and make a recording in your living room! It will be a worthwhile investment to spend a few hundred dollars, if necessary, to go to a professional studio and have a tape or CD made of which you can be proud and that reflects your best abilities. Percussion instruments, especially timpani, are difficult to record well, and the quality of the recording is a reflection of your integrity and care. A well made tape or CD can be used for many auditions.

If, after having sent your credentials, recommendations, and a well-made recording, you are not invited to audition and you feel you have the experience and ability to make a good showing at the audition, I suggest you call the personnel manager directly and gently insist that you be allowed to audition. He or she will try to convince you that you haven't a chance, but if you insist enough and make this person realize that you are willing to pay the expense to come and that you will not waste the time of the committee, he or she will most likely consent. If that doesn't work, call up the principal percussionist and tell him or her the same. I have known percussionists who just showed up at auditions and insisted that they be allowed to play. More than once a job has been won by someone who was not initially invited to the audition but had the determination to insist. It goes without saying that if you display this large amount of chutzpah you should be prepared to play a dynamite audition. Don't call anybody if you are not ready to win the audition, for if you do poorly you won't get a second chance and your reputation could be damaged.

Garnish with an outgoing personality (not overdone) on a generous platter of experience.

A Creative Recipe for the Improvising Vibist

Ed Saindon

Every great musical performance contains certain musical elements that contribute to the overall effectiveness and strength of the music. While someone's opinion about a specific musical presentation can be very subjective, there are individual musical factors that can greatly benefit a musical presentation. In this recipe, we will look at a partial list of some important musical ingredients and discuss how they can enhance a musical performance. Although the topics in this article could be applied to any instrumentalist, we will focus on the improvising vibist.

INGREDIENTS:
Dynamics
Articulation
Variety
Contrast
Simplicity
Drama

SERVES:
The improvising vibist, from beginners to advanced players.

Dynamics
One of the most crucial factors in any performance is the use of dynamics. Improvisation should be thought of as being analogous to speech. With that in mind, imagine how a person would sound if he or she spoke with no fluctuation of intensity, inflection, and volume. In most cases, the listener would undoubtedly lose interest and the delivery of the content would be severely diminished. This is also true in the delivery of a musical presentation.

There are many dynamic levels and, consequently, the vibist should not be afraid of using a very wide dynamic range. In general, the vibist should not be hesitant and timid with exaggerating the dynamics. I have never seen any vibist play who inserted too many changes in dynamics and had a dynamic range that was too excessive. The case has usually been the opposite. The overall consensus is that many vibists' performances have an absence of dynamics in general. If we lose dynamics on the vibraphone, we lose too much. A very common problem with many vibists is that they consistently play too loud. In trying to keep up with the volume of everyone else in the band, vibists often sacrifice this valuable dynamic range. The end result is a very flat sound, and the overall effectiveness of the performance is severely diminished.

Using dynamic contrast to create a rise and fall in a melodic line can greatly enhance a solo. Try playing a line without increasing or decreasing the volume at all, and then play it again with added dynamic contrast. The dynamics add shape and another dimension to the overall sound. Dynamic fluctuations on repeated, individual notes can also be an effective device in a melodic line. In essence, every note can have its own dynamic level. Some notes may be accented while other notes may be played ever so lightly, or "ghosted."

In solo playing, consideration should also be given to the various parts that make up the whole solo performance. The parts that serve as accompaniment should be played noticeably softer so as not to overshadow the melodic line. Specifically, the vibist should not be afraid to exaggerate the softness of a left-hand accompaniment part.

Articulation

Good articulation and clarity go hand in hand. The skillful use of dynamics won't do much good if the overall melodic line is a total blur. The deft and creative use of pedaling and dampening is essential in playing a melodic line or in executing an effective solo performance. In listening to a saxophone line, one can hear short notes, long notes, slurred notes, bent notes—the list goes on. For clarity, try to play the line a little more dry than wet, bearing in mind that much depends on the acoustics of the room in which you are playing.

After-pedaling or syncopated pedaling is a must for smooth, legato phrasing. The use of dampening is also essential in tapping the musical subtleties and nuance of which the instrument is capable of producing. Additionally, the use of dead strokes (where the mallet hits the note and stays on the bar so the note isn't allowed to ring) is an effective technique that, when combined with dampening, can simulate bending a note. Try to be as creative as possible with regard to articulation and phrasing. When you are playing, imagine that you are being recorded where every nuance is being heard. Strive to be very clear and clean in terms of articulation and phrasing.

Variety

No matter how good something is, too much of anything can negate the positive aspects. Whether it's a great series of motivic phrases, a strong solo technique in a solo rendition, or three great uptempo tunes in a row, a steady diet of anything can be a negative. In other words, repetition is fine and desirable up to a point; but after that point (and that point is subjective), boredom will undoubtedly set in upon the listener. Thus, in improvisation or in a solo performance, try to constantly change techniques so as to effectively hold the interest of the listener. Practicing one certain technique over and over to master it is fine in the practice room, but to do so on the stage is undesirable and diminishes the purity and direction of the music.

Contrast

Implied in the meaning of the word "variety" is the idea of contrast. To achieve a balanced performance, it helps to have a contrast of musical elements. For example, to appreciate an instrumentalist's technique, the performance is most effective with slowly played melodic passages as well as virtuosic feats of improvisation. With regard to solo playing, a rendition that is consistently too thick in texture will very often wear thin (pun unintended) on the listener. Likewise, a performance relying heavily on the rhythmic aspect will greatly benefit from moments with the focus being on melody or harmony. In other words, contrast maintains interest.

There are many areas where contrast can be applied. Here are a some possible contrasting musical elements: rhythmic density versus rhythmic sparseness; syncopation versus non-syncopation; playing "in" versus playing "out"; playing horizontally versus vertically; playing fast versus playing slow; playing with large intervals versus small intervals; playing a short phrase versus a long phrase; playing loud versus playing soft. The list is endless when it comes to incorporating contrast in one's playing.

Simplicity

In more ways than one, it is not easy to play in a simple manner. Sometimes we may get carried away in the heat of the moment, or we might start playing fast and too complicated in order to impress someone in the audience or even the band. The key is to focus on the music and to try to stay in control.

Getting caught up in the frantic pace of an intense solo can lead one to play beyond one's means and beyond the listener's comprehension. Playing in an uncomplicated way, on the other hand, aids in maintaining the focus and continuity of the improvised line or solo performance. If one listens to a great solo performance or masterful improvisation, one can often hear that, in actuality, much of the content is very simple. It is how everything is put together that makes the rendition strong; all the musical elements are there in perfect combination with each other, and every note is logical and played with clarity.

In solo playing, it is especially easy to lose oneself in a specific technique and to consequently lose the melodic thread of the composition. In such situations, try to remember that you are usually playing for a non-vibist audience. Your audience is not listening to a specific mallet technique, but rather to the melody, harmony, and rhythm of the composition. They are listening to the whole package and what kind of mood and story you are conveying. Consequently, focus on the music as opposed to technique; keep it simple; and at all times, try to project continuity, logic, and a nice flow throughout the piece.

Drama

Solo performances should have as much intensity and drama as a big band performance. Of course, the dynamic ranges, timbres, and textures are drastically different, but it is all relative. Again, the exaggeration of dynamics is important. Don't use up too much all at once; hold back the volume, intensity, and everything else. Use speed and volume sparingly; save some of it for later. Pace yourself. Use surprise in a performance. Make an unexpected dynamic change or a change in time feel. There are many ways to keep listeners involved, interested, and on the edge of their seat.

Conclusion

The above represents only a partial listing of musical ingredients in a recipe for an inherently strong performance. The important thing is to be analytical towards one's own playing and others' in terms of what makes a good performance. One suggestion I pass on to my students is to make up a musical checklist and place it on the music stand. As it is difficult to think of all the possibilities at the same time and play anything, I suggest choosing one or two of these musical elements and focus on them while practicing. Before long, the musical elements will be incorporated into the playing process naturally and consistently without consciously thinking of any specific musical element.

This recipe is only a partial list. Depending upon a player's tastes and dislikes, his or her list might be different from the next player. In addition, one player's various percentages of each ingredient and focus on a specific musical ingredient might differ from the next player. Vibists are encouraged to add their own musical ingredients to their personal recipes to make an overall strong and interesting performance. The recipe should be adjusted and fine tuned as each player evolves throughout his or her musical development.

A Well-Rounded Approach to Musical Growth

Dave Samuels

Growing as a musician involves much more than just developing technique. Here is a recipe for feeding such growth.

INGREDIENTS:
Self-awareness
Making it real
Harmony

SERVES:
All musicians.

Ingredient 1: 2 cups of self-awareness
Know what you've done: this will enable you to get a realistic understanding of how much you have grown by practicing, performing, and recording yourself.

1. Record yourself. Recording yourself is the most valuable tool you have. It is a musical mirror that allows you to hear what you really sound like. No more musical fantasies; reality is what's needed.

2. Have a journal that documents on a weekly basis what you have practiced, how long, and at what tempo.

3. List the rehearsals, performances, and types of ensembles you've played in.

Ingredient 2: 2 lbs. of "make it real"
Make sure that you spend time playing with accompaniment; use play-along CDs or, better yet, create your own background accompaniment. If you don't have a computer or a synthesizer with a sequencer, buy one. It's the best investment you can make. Playing with an accompaniment makes it real. You learn to listen and play. Record yourself with the accompaniment and hear how you really sound.

Ingredient 3: 12 oz. of harmony
1. Start to learn about basic harmony. Buy a beginning harmony book and play the examples in the book. Play basic chords. Learn to play major/minor triads, dominate 7th, and diminished 7th chords. These are the building blocks of the tonal musical language you need to learn in order to speak. Everyone, regardless of the instrument or style of music he or she plays, needs to know this. Once you understand and apply these basics principles you will be able to explore any type of music.

2. Study the music of the masters: Bach, Czerny, Gershwin, and Monk. Take the chord progressions from their pieces and write your own melodies.

3. Remember the C.I.A.: compose, improvise, and analyze. ➥

Recipe for Chart Reading

Casey Scheuerell

A chart is a road map, or visual sketch, designed to help you navigate a musical arrangement. It contains valuable information, mostly about what the other musicians are playing, as well as the layout of musical events that make up a particular piece. The drum part is largely improvised, and because of this, the more musical experience and knowledge you bring to reading, the more likely your chances for success.

Chart reading is an acquired skill, one that comes over time with practice. Being a good reader will make for greater work opportunities and enhance your ability to learn and perform music. The goal of this recipe is to give you a step-by-step, practical approach to chart reading.

INGREDIENTS:
The most important ingredients for successful sight-reading are the three F's:
Feel
Form
Fine
There is also one very special utensil required: a #2 lead pencil with eraser. (Never use ink!) A yellow highlighter can also be helpful.

SERVES:
This recipe serves intermediate to advanced drumset players and percussionists. Although it is primarily for non-classical musical styles, it contains tips that can prove helpful to classical percussionists.

The three F's are the foundation, and here's why:

Feel: This tells us the most important element of drumming. "If you ain't got the feel, you ain't going to deal." The "feel" gives us tempo and groove (i.e., straight or swing, half-time shuffle, mambo, samba or funk?) This will help you determine whether to use sticks, brushes, or mallets. It will give clues as to instrument selection: drumset, congas, shakers etc. Write your choices in the upper left-hand corner of the chart.

Form: Knowing the form allows for more faking—the fourth essential ingredient of chart reading. It gives you the extra security and leeway to be visually lost and find your way back: by listening. Most rehearsal letters mark the beginning of a new section of a form, as in, AABA, ABAB, 12-bar blues, Open Jam, etc. This allows for us to get our eyes out of the music and into communication. As a safety measure, make it a habit to know where the next rehearsal letter is on the page before taking your eyes away for a look around. When the arrangement hits the next section, you will know where to put your eyes.

Fine: (pronounced fee-nay) This is the musical term we use to announce the ending, as in "finish" or "final." No matter how well you read the notes on the page, the last thing everyone hears is the ending. Blowing the ending is like crashing the lead car on the final lap of the Daytona 500. Look ahead, memorize the ending. Maybe the coda is simply one-bar long but requires a difficult page turn to get there. Be ready. When you reach the *Fine*, go out looking good!

Sweeteners and Spice

Having used our main ingredients to make a solid foundation to work from, let's look at some finer points that will sweeten our results.

Scan: Begin at the top of the chart and proceeding to the very end, visually scan for specific instructions. Look for:

Repeats: Find repeats of all kinds, brackets, 1st and 2nd endings, D.S., D.C. al Coda. Figure out how it all works. Use a pencil or yellow highlighter to mark difficult-to-see repeats. (Be sure it's okay with the leader to mark your parts.)

Dynamics: Look for dynamic markings. A drummer who can bring a band up or down to the chart dynamic markings is a real pro.

Figures and Note Densities: The most common pitfall drummers make is to go here when first handed a chart. If scan time is limited, the three F's win over the particulars of figure interpretation. Most often it is not essential for the drummer to read every figure. In fact, letting a few go by shows good taste. If time permits, you can begin to think about set-ups and hits. If you do nail a tricky passage, you'll make an impression.

Solos: Don't let the word "solo" scare you. Is the solo short (two bars) or long (a full chorus)? If soloing causes anxiety, try to relax and work outward from the groove and what you are naturally hearing and already playing. A simple, embellished time feel can be as effective as flash, and will often be more musical.

Time Changes, Metric Modulations, and Weird Stuff: This speaks for itself. Sometimes you will find things that may need clarification. If you don't know ask, but try to keep questions to a minimum and to the point. If you find you are missing the last page of a chart, you may want to bring that up before the show begins. If there is a difficult transition to make, ask if you can rehearse that spot before working the entire piece.

I hope this recipe helps you in your reading quest. Successfully navigating a difficult chart can be exhilarating. It gives you a chance to "test your metals" and see what you're made of. Plan on many failures before you begin having successes. To be sure, just when you think you've seen it all, someone will throw you a curve. It is a lifelong process. Good luck and have fun! ➮

A Tasteful Concert Bass Drum

James A. Sewrey

A concert bass drum is a musical instrument, and as such it needs to be properly manipulated according with its design and function. True, it's a non-pitched instrument, but when it's properly tuned for its size and functional use, sounded with an appropriate mallet or mallets, and played with musical sensitivity, the concert bass drum is a musical instrument, and very much an integral part of a concert/symphonic band or orchestra's instrumentation.

INGREDIENTS:
One concert bass drum with two quality heads properly mounted and tuned
One sturdy support stand
Selected mallets/sticks
A height-adjustable padded table stand for the mallets/sticks and any needed ancillary percussion instrument
External mute(s).

SERVES:
Concert band/orchestra percussionists and listening audiences alike.

Preparation: Tensioning and Tuning of the Heads
Both heads are to be evenly brought under tension around the perimeter of the drum by adjusting each tension rod to raise or lower the pitch-point of the head to match the pitch-point at the tension rod directly opposite, across the head. This can be done by tapping the head, adjacent to the tension-rod, at an equal distance from the rim of the shell (about three inches), using a hard-felt or yarn mallet head.

Once each head has been adjusted to be in tune with itself, adjust the batter head to the desired tonal pitch-point, and then adjust the receiving head to an interval pitch-point of a third or fourth below that of the batter head's tonal pitch-point. (A bass drum head that has lost its tonal vibrancy/elasticity needs to be replaced, and a proper mounting, adjustment, and "break-in" procedure followed.)

Mix in: Selected Mallets
Not just any kind of mallet will do; likewise, just any way that it's manipulated, or anywhere it may strike the batter head, will not do. One needs to take into consideration the character of the composition when selecting the proper mallet(s) to be used in articulating the written part on the size and tuning of the concert bass drum that is used: the composition of the mallet handle (kind, thickness, size, and length) and the mallet head's material/covering and degree of hardness. Then there's the manner in which the mallet is held/gripped (firmly/loosely) and manipulated to articulate a legato, staccato, marcato, or a sustained sound, using

either a hinge or rotation action of the wrist with an up-down or down-up stroke of the mallet to "sound" the drum's head.

Add: The Choice of Beating Area, the Manner of Head Control, and Selective Muting

Three basic beating areas on the surface of the batter head can be used to effectively articulate notational-durations and add tonal-shading by playing: 1. near the center of the head, 2. near the edge of the head, and 3. midway between the center and edge of the drumhead, thus adding musical nuance to the written part for the concert bass drum.

In conjunction with the "sounding" of a concert bass drum is the manipulative interplay that takes place between the right-hand mallet stroke and the use of the left hand and/or right knee to dampen/muffle the vibrating heads to control the duration of their sound in keeping with the character of the composition. This coordinative and sensitive manipulation is an art in itself, providing finesse to the phrasing.

External mutes are used as desired, or as designated in the concert bass drum part, to accommodate the character of the composition. One such mute is a towel-pad unit, and another is a mechanical device; both are attached to the drum's shell. The towel-pad unit is used by manually controlling the amount of material that touches the batter head, and the mechanical device, which is fixed to the counterhoop of the receiving head, has its muting pressure adjusted, as desired.

Decide: What Size Concert Bass Drum to Use, Where to Place, and How to Position

Like with the other instruments in a concert/symphonic band or orchestra, the size and placement of a concert bass drum and its positioning (upright, at an angle, or laid flat), is predicated upon the particular ensemble's instrumentation and the musical compositions being performed, their historical significance and character, the performance area's physical surroundings, and the acoustics in the physical area, with regard for ensemble blend, balance, and precision between the various sections.

Make Use Of: A Properly Prepared Support Stand, Body Position, and Padded Mallet Table.

A concert bass drum support stand needs to be sturdy—its metal-to-metal parts securely fastened and its hanging straps or padded material securely fastened to the drum's shell or stand's frame. Depending upon the character of the music being played, the player either addresses the concert bass drum from a standing position or seated on a stool. The use of a height-adjustable padded table is a necessary accessory for holding the concert bass drum performance mallets, and for the occasional use of small concert percussion instruments such as tambourine, castanets, maracas, finger cymbals, or claves.

Nurture the Playing With: A Pinch of Finesse, a Dash of Sensitivity, a Whole Lot of Creativity, and Cook with Imagination

Embrace the music, using one or a combination of the performance factors to make music with a concert bass drum. Don't be satisfied with just "beating" the notated rhythm of any written bass drum part. ➝●

Drumset Balance

Ed Shaughnessy

There is an element of drumset "balance" that is often missing at high school and college-level events. Here, then, are recipes for balancing the drumset in jazz and rock situations in terms of dynamics.

INGREDIENTS:

Jazz
80% ride cymbal rhythm and hi-hat with foot
20% steady bass drum with snare accents

Rock
80% bass and snare drum beat
20% ride cymbal or hi-hat with stick

SERVES:
All drumset players

In jazz playing, one must "feather" the bass drum, which is a necessary sound for jazz drumming. It provides a "bottom" to the drum sound, and although it is very subtle, it completes the desired effect. In big band work it is a key to a full sound from the player.

If the drummer does not maintain the bass drum and attempts to drive the band with the ride cymbal and the hi-hat foot only, the result is a thin sound. In a small group the use of the bass drum is not as critical, but most skilled jazz drummers do play the bass drum and many esteemed bass players have said that they prefer it.

The lack of dynamics in many players' bass drum control is often the culprit. When a band director hears a heavy 4/4 on the bass drum, he often says, "No bass drum." This is understandable. What he *should* say is, "Practice for a lighter touch on the bass drum in this rhythm."

In rock playing, however, the bass drum enjoys an even, "up front" sound with the snare drum. The bass drum is usually played "heel-up" on the pedal (whereas feathering is usually best done with a "heel-down" position).

Latin drumming usually has an "all even" dynamic between hands and feet. Good control of all three types of playing should be the goal of every drummer. ➟●

If You Can Sing It You Can Play It

Kristen Shiner McGuire

Goal: To more easily digest new coordination patterns between hands and feet.

INGREDIENTS:
Your voice (sweet or salty)
Four limbs (flesh and bone)
Drumset (any style)
Sticks (avoid chopsticks—too thin)

SERVES:
Drumset players and teachers of any age or ability.

The ideas in these recipes are designed to act like catalysts for learning—like an enzyme or baking soda speeding up the process. The first formula is Composite Learning: hearing/feeling the whole without having to think about separate parts.

Let's say you want to learn the bossa nova using three limbs. You've learned the bossa nova clave in the left hand and steady eighths in the right hand, and now you want to add the bass drum; first on beats 1 and 3. Isolate the tricky part: left-hand clave with the right foot. Look at how the notes line up on paper and name the parts: "both," "hand," and "foot." Then say the composite pattern, *in rhythm*, using those words: "Both - - hand foot - hand - foot - hand - foot hand - -." Say and play these parts, either on the set or just sitting in a chair (tap your foot and hit your thigh).

After you get that, use the same process with the standard bass drum pattern: 1, & of 2, 3, & of 4. The verbalization would then be: "Both - - both foot - hand foot foot - hand foot foot hand - -." Be patient and make sure your limbs are actually doing what your voice is saying!

You can use this composite approach with any two limbs in any style. To begin the process, isolate the most syncopated part of a particular beat and see how the notation lines up with one of the other parts on paper. After you've figured out the verbalization and practiced it, add the ostinato part back in (e.g., steady eighths with the right hand on the cymbal for the bossa nova).

Some composite rhythms are commonly used for basic polyrhythms. For example, two against three may be said as "both - right left right -", or "not - dif-fi-cult -." Three against four may be said, " both - - right left - right - left right - -" or "eat - - the gosh - darn - spin-ach - -" (the latter is healthier). You may want to develop a set of your own catchy phrases; some of the best recipes start with improvisation (not including the pineapple on pizza thing, however).

The second formula is especially useful for teachers using the rote method for teaching drum-set patterns. If the student is not ready to read syncopations, the rhythms can be presented as verbal phrases and learned first by ear. For example, when I teach the mambo bell pattern (played on the bell of the ride cymbal), I use, "Don't – go – walk-in - a-lone -at-night - no no -." The student doesn't need to understand the counting, just how it sounds—by itself at first, then against a steady pulse or ostinato, which the teacher can play with the student.

A useful phrase for the standard jazz ride pattern is, "You - swing it, I - swing it." Have the student say it over and over with you so he or she gets the right feel and spacing of notes. The jazz feel has a particular flavor that can only be absorbed by repeated, active listening.

For more advanced learners, the voice can be used to sing one part while playing another. This works well in developing jazz independence. Take a melodic rhythm played against the swing ride cymbal pattern—usually a short, syncopated phrase using quarter and swing eighth notes. "Sing" the phrase (on one pitch) as a horn player would, using the idiomatic phrasing of long and short sounds. Then sing it slowly, in time, while playing quarter notes on the ride cymbal. Think triplets, and listen for the space between the notes. Then stop and just play the swing beat slowly. Try singing the phrase against the cymbal pattern. This may be difficult, but repeated practice will achieve success.

A helpful ingredient in this recipe is a metronome. If you can sing the phrase with only quarter notes on the cymbal, you're still developing a good sense of style and timing. When you can sing against the ride beat without varying it, it means the latter is fully ingrained, and you can tackle any rhythm!

The last step is to play the vocal phrase with your left hand on the snare drum; then the right foot on the bass drum, then the melody between the snare and bass drums—all against the ride beat in the right hand.

As you can see, your voice is a key ingredient for becoming a quick-rise learner and a tasteful drummer. Use all your senses to enhance your style—whether spicy, smooth, jumpin' bean, or rumba! You've got all the elements you need at your fingertips. ➤●

Developing a Unique Voice

Dick Sisto

Before we begin "cooking" this recipe, let us consider one of the greatest musicians and composers of all time, J.S. Bach. Most people are aware that Bach wrote complex music, which was often composed of contrapuntal, modulating lines that incorporated chromaticism, logical melodic and harmonic development, and rhythmic forward motion. It is also common knowledge that Bach, whenever he performed, took liberties (i.e., improvised) with his music. His "voice" was so ingrained in his being that he possessed a freedom that allowed him to spontaneously recreate a written piece of music.

This was also true of Charlie Parker. "Bird" would seldom play one of the many complex tunes he wrote in exactly the same way. Like his improvisations on the tunes, he was always looking for ever new interpretations. Parker, incidentally, was a great admirer and disciple of Bach. The bebop that Parker helped create bore striking similarities to Bach's compositions, especially in relation to elements like chord changes, leading tones, and thematic development.

Okay, let's begin cooking. Here are the ingredients we will need to develop an individual voice on our instrument.

INGREDIENTS:
Technical proficiency
Good ears
Selected seasonings (see below)

SERVES:
All improvising musicians.

The first ingredient is technical proficiency, or relative mastery of our instrument. This means that we must be able to execute whatever our improvisation dictates. It will often require practice to achieve this, but having technical proficiency means we have practiced and become skilled at covering all the fundamental scales, arpeggios, melodies, chords, and rhythms that will allow us to add new ingredients to our musical "stew."

The second main ingredient is the development of our ears. We must be able to internalize the music so that, later, we can learn to play what we hear and thus express our own voice. This is achieved by, first of all, listening to the great recordings of the masters of jazz. Who should we listen to? The answer is simple and in the form of a question. Ask yourself, "Who do I like?" Everyone has personal preferences. If you don't know the answer to the question, then you must develop a passion, if that is possible, for the music in general.

Begin the process by listening to many great jazz recordings. Remember, all of the greatest jazz has already been played, and when it comes to the modern idiom we can look to the 1950s and '60s as the era from which to absorb the best of the best.

Now that we have some of the main ingredients in the mix, we need to add the seasoning and spices, which will give the recipe a unique flavor. One way in which we can do this is by practicing the art of *emulating* rather than *imitating* the jazz masters we are studying. This is done by listening to a specific "lick" or "line" from a master and then changing and adapting it to the way we "hear it" in the context of our own improvisation, thereby "making it our own." In this way we will develop a style or "voice" that reflects influences without sounding as though we are imitating, which can be a kind of jazz plagiarism.

Everyone loves a bit of hot sauce or peppers in the mix. One way in which we can do this musically in our improvisation is to emphasize the rhythmic element as much as the melodic or harmonic development. Sometimes, excitement, transition, or climax can be achieved with a very simple, even repetitive rhythmic figure. A strong rhythmic pulse that swings hard and propels the notes with a sense of urgency is essential to any good improvisation.

We shouldn't forget another facet of music that is often left out of the jazz improvisation recipe: dynamics. The use of dynamics within a jazz solo indicates a high degree of musical maturity in the player. The dynamics should be added to the form and structure of the solo when needed. They should never be an end in themselves.

We need to add two more ingredients to this mixture: One is called phrasing and the other is "feel." They work hand in hand and create a delicious "flow" that makes the entire recipe work.

Finally, if there is no emotion behind the notes, all of it will be for naught. There will be no communication with the audience and consequently they will not be able to enjoy the banquet.

Practicing and Playing the Drumset

Ed Soph

If you cannot play something immediately to your or your teacher's satisfaction it is because the material is *new*, not *difficult*. New exercises and techniques require new ways of thinking, hearing, and moving. The more you think about what you're doing and how you're doing it, the better your problem-solving technique becomes. And that is what practicing is about: developing the self-awareness to recognize your musical and technical limitations and learning how to overcome those limitations.

INGREDIENTS:
1 drumset
1 pair of sticks or brushes
1 metronome
1 pair of ears
1 brain

SERVES:
Drummers at all levels.

Practice your musical and technical weaknesses, not your strengths. If you sound good when you are practicing, you are not really practicing.

Make practicing playing. Movement skills are learned by repetition, by trial and error; by learning to correct, to adjust, and to adapt while actually playing. By applying musical frameworks of form, style, tempo, dynamics, rhythm, and melody to your practicing, you will practice imaginatively and prepare yourself for the demands of the bandstand.

Hear everything you are playing, whether it is repetitive or non-repetitive, written or improvised.

Practice with a metronome to develop your sense of consistent time.

Avoid practicing in your dynamic "comfort zone." As a general approach, practice exercises very softly as well as loudly—and everything in between!

Break exercises into their components. Play individual parts before attempting to play the complete pattern. Play individual measures before attempting to play the complete exercise. This allows your mind to understand the process of playing the exercise. It is your brain, not your hands and feet, that plays the drums.

"Control" comes from degrees of looseness, not tightness.

Practicing new material slowly is the quickest way to learn it. Practicing slowly gives you the opportunity to think about what you are doing. If you can't play it at quarter note = 40–50, you haven't really mastered the exercise.

"Sing" parts before you play them. "Sing" one part while playing another.

Be patient. Remember, progress is doing, not completing.

Don't stop if you play something "wrong." If what you played is in time, it is an improvisation, not a mistake! Go with the flow. Let what your brain initially wanted to play come out. That's you playing. Work your way to the original exercise. In the end, you'll have some variations of the exercise because you allowed yourself to make mistakes musically while practicing. The same process occurs when you actually play music in a band, so get used to it!

When you hear an accomplished musician, always ask yourself, "Why does he/she sound so good?" If you learn to hear and identify the good attributes in others' playing, you will be able to bring those qualities to your own playing.

Practice thoughtfully. The accomplished players are those who have invested the most time practicing, playing, and thinking about their instrument and the music. They are also the ones who have listened thoroughly to the musical repertoire. They are the players who have developed their ears just as well as their hands and feet.

Explore the musical history of the drumset. That will help you understand the present and guide you in charting your own musical future.

Technique is like handwriting. We all learned to make the same basic letterforms when we were taught to write. Yet now we all possess unique styles of writing because we took those basic, fundamental forms and personalized them, thus creating our own "hand." So it is with drumming techniques. Learn and internalize the basic forms, let your musical imagination go to work, and you will find your own musical "hand."

Finally, remember that you sound the way that you move. Drumming is motion. Smooth, in-time motions (strokes) produce smooth, in-time rhythms and sounds. Jerky, out-of-time motions produce the equivalent sounds. The quality of the silent part of the stroke (the upstroke) determines the quality of the downstroke, the part that produces the sound. Silence in time produces sound in time. ➤●

Improved Snare Drum Solo Scores

Gary Stith

When solo festival time approaches, here are a few "ingredients" to assist you in helping your snare drummers "cook up" that monumental Superior rating and benefit from a significant amount of personal improvement along the way.

INGREDIENTS:
Snare drum
Appropriate sticks
Knowledge of rudiments
Understanding of style
Observance of dynamics

SERVES:
Drummers preparing snare drum solos for contests.

Step 1: Provide Your Own Well-Tuned Snare Drum. Many students lose points every year because they plan (or simply "hope") to use the festival's provided drum. Unfortunately, there is no guarantee that this instrument will have been tuned since the Eisenhower administration and may quite possibly render a sound that is something far short of the "crisp" desired response. Help the student tune his or her (or your school's) drum and seek assistance, if necessary, from a percussionist colleague.

Step 2: Use Appropriate Size Sticks. Just as you wouldn't even consider sending a trumpet player to a solo festival performing the Haydn Trumpet Concerto on a "super-screecher jet-tone" mouthpiece, be sure not to send a snare drummer performing a rudimental solo on model 7A drumset sticks. Just as a shallow cup mouthpiece produces a thinner, more piercing tone, light and skinny snare sticks also produce a thin sound that is inappropriate for playing rudimental and most concert solos. Size 2B, Firth SD1, or the equivalent are best suited for most festival solo work.

Step 3: Avoid Playing Too Close to the Rim. Tone quality is the determining factor here. The best sounding spot on most snare drums is usually about an inch off center. Though it is indeed easier to play *p* or *pp* dynamic levels (especially rolls) at a spot about one inch from the rim, the tone quality of many drums becomes very thin at that location on the head and also often lacks sufficient snare response. You may move slightly closer to the rim for softer passages, but be sure the tone of the drum is still full and results in ample snare response. Let your musical ear be your guide.

Step 4: Prepare Appropriate Rudiments for the Grade Level of the Solo. Many students lose points during this portion of their audition for a couple of basic reasons. First, they fail to realize that there is a list of *specific* rudiments to prepare. See your state manual for the requirements and provide each student with a list of those rudiments well in advance. Second, your students must understand that the rudiment portion of their score will reflect how well they perform each of these elements of snare drumming, and not just their basic knowledge of them. (Note that this is a different philosophy from that of the scale requirement category on wind and string instruments upon which all the points will generally be granted even if the tone quality is poor and the intonation is suspect!) Regularly listen to these rudiments as students are preparing them, and be sure they are observing correct stickings, accents, and approximate required tempi. Again, consult your state manual for all of these specifications.

Step 5: If Required, Diligently Prepare the Long "Open-Close-Open" Roll. There is a reason that, in a number of states, this rudiment is required at various levels of solo difficulty. To perform the long roll with the desired control and execution is quite difficult and requires a long time to develop. Unfortunately, many students rarely practice it until a few evenings prior to their audition, and as a result, lose unnecessary points. The Long Roll should be practiced with correct stick positions throughout (high to low to high), the second "bounce" of each stick must always match the first in volume (or perhaps be played slightly louder, as was traditional a number of years ago), the space between strokes must be even, the closed portion of the roll must be played in a relaxed multiple-bounce style with no pulsations, and the "transitions" must be *seamless*. Instructors are encouraged to listen to student progress on this roll regularly throughout the weeks and/or months of solo audition preparation.

Step 6: All Flams Must be Performed Correctly. Flams must sound as if saying the word "flam." Rarely should they sound like saying "fa-lam" (too open) or "fam" (popped or flat flams). To do this consistently takes careful attention to stick positions and conscientious practice. Poorly executed flams are unacceptable.

Step 7: Perform the Solo in the Appropriate Style. Rudimental snare drum solos must always be performed in a rudimental "open roll" style. Unless specifically designated by the composer, "closed" orchestral rolls, ruffs, and drags are unacceptable when playing a rudimental solo. On the other hand, "open" style is also generally unacceptable when performing a concert solo. In determining which style to employ, printed rudimental sticking patterns, specific roll requests (5, 7, 9, etc.), and even the title ("Heating the Rudiments," "Connecticut Halftime," etc.) may often indicate the "open" style. In recent years, some states have thoughtfully begun indicating the appropriate style (rudimental vs. concert or orchestral) of each solo in their state manuals.

Step 8: Observe All Printed Sticking Patterns. The stickings are written in a solo to encourage ambidexterity, to raise or lower the level of performance difficulty, and are one significant element of snare drum *phrasing*. In addition, if the solo is rudimental in nature, the performer is expected to play appropriate stickings even if not always specifically designated. An example of this is the level 2 solo "Yankee Doodle Paradiddle" by G.W. Lotzenhiser (*Classic Festival Solos for Solo Snare Drum* published by Warner Brothers). Though there is a lack of printed sticking patterns in this piece, the title indicates that the groups of *alla breve* eighth notes must utilize the sticking pattern of the single paradiddle.

Step 9: Carefully Observe All Printed Dynamics. This, of course, is no great revelation, but dynamic contrast is especially critical in most drum solos because of the lack of a melodic line. The performance of a snare solo with virtually no dynamic variation is about as "engaging" as listening to random dots and dashes on the telegraph! Plead, beg, bargain, or do whatever necessary to coerce your students into taking dynamics seriously. For some percussionists, the use of a whip and a chair may prove to be effective motivators! ➤●

What Are You Prepared To Do?

John Tafoya

Some of you may recognize the title of this recipe from the movie *The Untouchables*, in which Sean Connery's character is asking what Elliot Ness (Kevin Costner) is "prepared to do" to determine his level of commitment in capturing Al Capone. This comment can easily be applied to the success of an orchestral musician's professional life.

INGREDIENTS:
Complete dedication
Commitment
Focus
Solid work ethic
Determination to succeed (tunnel vision toward your goal)

SERVES:
The serious high school student, college music major, and professional musician.

What should you be prepared to do? The answer is: *anything* and *everything* to advance your knowledge of your instrument, repertoire, personal performance, and recognizing your musical purpose in any ensemble. This translates into a tremendous amount of practicing, score study, listening to recordings, and seeking out as many performance opportunities as possible. This may also mean participating in less than ideal musical situations in order to gain the necessary experience.

Today's music major rarely makes the jump from school to a top orchestra job. It is quite normal to start out in a smaller "per-service" orchestra or an orchestra with a shorter season. This initial professional experience can be quite frustrating as your orchestra might only rehearse on the weekends and present one performance. Due to the limited rehearsal time and inconsistent orchestral personnel, the conductor might only be able to rehearse and perform the music with one consistent interpretation. This delivers a decent concert but it does not encourage or expose the musicians to flexible music making. Major symphony orchestras will average five rehearsals with at least three concerts each week. For certain programs, very little (if any) rehearsal time will be available. Successful orchestral musicians have to keep up with this fast pace.

In addition to this musical scenario, some musicians will audition for an "extras list"— hoping for an opportunity to perform as an extra player in a larger orchestra. Others will teach or take a non-musical job to supplement their income. Young musicians may have to juggle all of these employment opportunities and, at the same time, be practicing and studying to improve their playing level and honing their audition skills. It is quite easy to lose focus during this time in your early professional life. Stick with it and don't give up! You may be surrounded by jaded musicians who have already relinquished their dreams of getting a better job. Don't let their attitude drag you down. It is easy to dwell on the negative aspects of your current situation. Establish a regular routine that includes the daily learning of new excerpts and continue to focus and prepare for the next orchestral audition.

Auditioning for a coveted spot in a major orchestra is very similar to training for an Olympic event. A great deal of attention must be directed toward every detail: time/tempo, intonation, dynamics, the proper character/style, and individual personality. Many younger musicians are now being trained to play from "letter A to letter B," studying only the required excerpts for any given audition. However, there also seems to be a trend at auditions to perform in a way "not to get caught"—performing everything in a clean and perfect manner. These interpretations are often void of any musical personality. Although every musician has his or her own "audition tactics," my approach was to play solid preliminary and semi-final rounds. If I reached the final round, and felt confident with my playing, I would take musical "risks" (exaggerating dynamics, phrasing, etc.) to try to set my performance apart from the other finalists.

Every orchestral audition serves as an incredible learning experience. Keeping a journal of your experiences is quite helpful. Also be sure to perform for a variety of friends, colleagues, and professionals. Value their feedback and guidance. With perseverance and determination, you will eventually land that dream job.

When I joined the National Symphony Orchestra in the summer of 1999, some of our morning rehearsals at Wolf Trap were so hot and muggy we were unable to rehearse the entire works. Fortunately, I had previous performance experience with most of the NSO's summer repertoire. Imagine performing Berlioz's "Symphonie Fantastique" and Holst's "The Planets" with very little rehearsal time! That's exactly what happened. Years of studying and practical performance experience certainly paid off in this instance. The summer performances were a success.

Before each orchestral season I also made it a habit to listen to recordings (featuring the same conductor and work to be performed, if possible) of unfamiliar music before the first rehearsal. If the repertoire included a premiere, or a piece that had not been recorded, I would study the score to mark in necessary cues and other useful information. Gathering this information allowed me to be "concert ready" by the first rehearsal. There were also instances in which errors were found that saved me a potentially uncomfortable moment during a rehearsal. In studying a work by composer Kalevi Aho, I determined that my timpani part was missing several crucial measures of music. If I had found this out at the first rehearsal, I would have had to re-adjust a handful of tuning changes and other musical details. Finding this error ahead of time saved me several hours of practicing and a frustrating first rehearsal.

The journey of a professional orchestral musician can be a long and tumultuous ride. Focusing on short-term and long-term goals while taking advantage of all performance opportunities will add to your "total package" as a successful orchestral musician. Tunnel vision, determination, hard work, and perseverance will ultimately form the building blocks of your success. ➤●

Private Lessons for the Beginner—Like a Well-Balanced Meal

Garwood Whaley

Developing a firm foundation on snare drum is a great way to begin the study of percussion instruments including drumset, keyboard percussion, and timpani. Establishing good technique, learning to read, developing the ability to play with another person, increasing good practice habits, understanding how to listen and adjust or correct problems, acquiring a concept of dynamics, and being able to control tempo are all fundamental to becoming a good musician, regardless of the instrument.

Each lesson should be comprehensive by including:

- technical exercises (rudiments and stick control exercises)
- duets (to introduce students to ensemble playing)
- prepared reading (assigned from the last lesson)
- multiple drum studies (as an introduction to drumset, multiple percussion, and timpani)
- sight-reading
- creativity study (student composition assignment)

INGREDIENTS:
Practice pad
drumsticks
motivated student

SERVES:
All students interested in drumming and percussion.

Menu
Establishing good hand position is the most important first step in developing good technique on snare drum. Here are suggestions for establishing good hand position.

Hand Position
There are two snare drum grips: the Matched Grip and the Traditional Grip.

Matched Grip: Both the right and left sticks are held alike when this grip is used. The stick is grasped between the fleshy part of the thumb and the first joint of the index finger (figure 1). The butt of the stick fits naturally in the main crease of the palm and the remaining three fingers wrap firmly around the stick (figure 2). Notice that the stick is equally supported by the thumb and index finger (figure 1) and the last three fingers (figure 3). Note carefully the complete grip (figure 4).

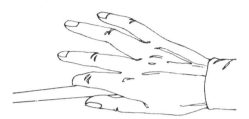

Fig 1. The stick is held between the fleshy part of the thumb and the first joint of the index finger. This provides 50% of the grip.

Fig. 2. The stick fits naturally in the main crease of the palm. The last three fingers wrap firmly around the stick.

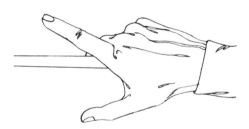

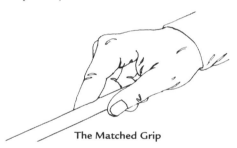

The Matched Grip

Fig. 3. The last three fingers wrap firmly around the stick. This provides 50% of the grip.

Fig. 4.

Fig. 5. Traditional Grip: When this grip is utilized, the right hand is held exactly the same as the matched grip. The left hand, however, is quite different. The butt of the stick is grasped in the crotch of the thumb and index finger. The stick rests on the flat of the fourth finger between the first and second joint. The index and third finger lie across the top of the stick. The fifth finger rests beneath the fourth finger. Note that the wrist is curved in toward the body.

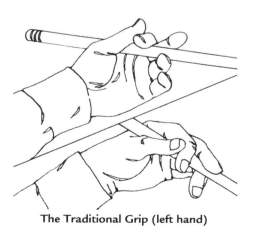

The Traditional Grip (left hand)

(**from** *Primary Handbook for Snare Drum*, Meredith Music Publications)

Body Position: The drum or practice pad should be at waist level. Both forearms are parallel to the ground. The sticks should form a V on the drum approximately three or four inches from the far rim.

Appetizer

Rudiments and stick control exercises are the bread and butter of technique. Practicing technique-developing exercises daily, and then reviewing them during the lesson, is an important part of any lesson.

Salad

Duets provide students with pre-ensemble performance experience by allowing them to play with another person. Duets also improve sight-reading skills since they force students to play without stopping to correct mistakes. Students should prepare (outside of the lesson) and play both parts of a duet during each lesson with their teacher.

Main Dish

Prepared reading studies should be a major part of each lesson. Assign a new reading study during each lesson to be prepared by the student prior to the next lesson. The reading study should be critiqued by the teacher for rhythmic accuracy, tempo, dynamics, embellishments (flams, ruffs, etc.), phrasing, and overall musical style.

Cheese Plate

Since percussionists are often required to play on a combination of instruments, multiple drum studies help prepare students to read more than one line of music and to apply appropriate sticking patterns. Lessons should begin with two drums (or practice pads) and gradually add a third and then a fourth. This will help in moving to timpani, drumset, and multiple percussion.

Dessert

Sight-reading is by far the most difficult aspect of music performance for all instrumentalists. Providing short, not-too-difficult sight reading materials during each lesson will greatly assist the student in developing this most important skill. Insist that students play from the beginning to the end of a piece without stopping!

Coffee/Tea

Playing a musical instrument is a creative art. So why not develop the student's creativity to its fullest potential? Incorporating a short, four- or eight-measure composition assignment as a part of each lesson can greatly stimulate creativity. Use whatever level of rhythmic reading you are working on as the basis for this assignment. If, for instance, you are working on eighth notes and rests in 3/4 time, have the student compose a short four- or eight-measure "composition" using these same rhythms, rests, and time signature. Review the work during the next lesson and have the student play it for you. This is also a great way to determine whether or not the student understands the reading material that you are presently working on.

Summary

Here's an *approximate* breakdown of a well-constructed private lesson:

- 30% technical exercises
- 10% duets
- 30% prepared reading
- 10% multiple drum studies
- 10% sight-reading

- 10% creativity study
- This breakdown works well in a one hour lesson. However, if teaching thirty minute lessons, it may be necessary to rotate some of these topics between lessons. For example, alternating duets with multiple drum studies every other lesson.

Bon appétit! ➤

Frame Drum Chops with Spicy Rudimental Marinade

B. Michael Williams

With this recipe, you can create a sumptuous world percussion cuisine using many ingredients you may already have on hand, including good old-fashioned rudiments applied to frame drums. The marinade takes time in order for all ingredients to properly marry, but the results are well worth the effort. An added bonus is that this dish actually *burns calories!*

INGREDIENTS:

Any frame drum (*tar, riq, bendir, bodhran, etc.*)
Arabic Tambourine by Mary Ellen Donald (San Francisco: Mary Ellen Books, 1985) or any source of traditional Arabic rhythms for frame drums.
PAS International Drum Rudiments (especially roll and drag patterns; available free at www.pas.org)
Stick Control by George Lawrence Stone (Randolph, MA: George B. Stone & Son, Inc., 1963)
A few standard rudimental snare drum solos
Frame drum solos, ensembles, and improvisations

SERVES:

Intermediate to advanced percussionists with a practical knowledge of traditional rudiments and an interest in applying them to developing frame drumming techniques.

Among the first drums I encountered from the African continent were the frame drums from the desert areas of North Africa. The *tar, bendir, riq,* and ancestors of the Irish *bodhran* originate in the countries that border the Mediterranean Sea (Morocco, Algeria, Tunisia, Libya, and Egypt) and throughout the Middle East. In many of these instruments, I saw the ancestry of our western orchestral percussion instruments. The Moroccan *bendir,* with its single gut snare running along the underside of the head, is quite possibly an ancestral prototype of the snare drum, and the Egyptian *riq* is a predecessor of the tambourine.

I was struck by the amazing variety of sounds that could be produced from a simple skin stretched across a cylindrical frame. Further, I saw a striking similarity between the vocalizations used to represent the various strokes in this drumming ("dum," "tak," "ka," "cha") and our own traditional snare drum rudiments ("flam," "ruff," "paradiddle," "ratamacue"). Inspired by the eloquently virtuosic performances of Glen Velez, I obtained a few instruments and familiarized myself with some traditional Arabic rhythms through a wonderful book by Mary Ellen Donald titled *Arabic Tambourine: A Comprehensive Course in Techniques and Performance for the Tambourine, Tar, and Mazhar.* I began collecting rhythms and grooves in a little notebook, and eventually incorporated some into solo compositions for my students.

Many of these solos use a rhythmic language derived in part from my studies in rudimental drumming.

I usually begin working with students on frame drums once they have developed a strong technique on snare drum and have performed some substantial solo works for that instrument. After introducing the student to the basic frame drum strokes ("dum," "tak," and "slap"), we explore some practical applications of these sounds through a few traditional rhythms such as Malfuf (dum - - dum - - slap -), Saudi (dum - - slap - - slap -), Maqsum (dum slap – slap dum – slap -) and Masmudi (dum – dum – tak tak - tak dum – tak tak – tak tak -) among others.

Once the student has grasped the basic techniques and can play some fundamental rhythms *with good sound quality* (vitally important!), we are ready to add embellishments such as drags and rolls. A solid background in rudimental drumming is especially helpful here, and I always find it appropriate to review the standard rudiments at this point.

No matter which frame drum a student chooses to play (*tar, riq,* or *bodhran*), the rolls are executed in the same manner; the ring and middle fingers of each hand act as the stroke and subsequent bounce of the snare drum stick. In my compositions for frame drums, this is usually notated with "43 43," etc. beneath the roll notations to indicate the 4th and 3rd fingers respectively. I usually start with the 5-stroke roll using a L R L – R L R sticking:

43	43	4	–	43	43	4	–
L	R	L	–	R	L	R	–

and progress through the 7- and 9-stroke rolls. The 6-stroke roll introduces consecutive (LR) 4th finger accents:

43	43	4	4
L	R	L	R

as does the 10-stroke roll

43	43	43	43	4	4
L	R	L	R	L	R

The student continues in like manner through all roll rudiments. The drag rudiments (ruffs, drag taps, drag paradiddles, lesson 25, and ratamacues) are especially effective in developing a repertoire of techniques for embellishing improvisations and increasing dexterity.

Years ago, I developed a daily regimen for maintaining technical facility on snare drum using the first 13 pages of George Lawrence Stone's *Stick Control*. I assigned a day of the week to each column so I completed the first 13 pages (effectively comprising the essential elements of the book) in one week. I highly recommend this practice regimen for any student or professional interested in building or rebuilding a solid drumming technique. It also happens to be highly effective in building frame drum facility, control, and endurance. Any pattern can be assigned various combinations of strokes (using "dum," "tak," "slap," etc.) to create rhythmic "melodies."

The exercises begin on page 5 with "Single Beat Combinations," so label the two columns on that page "Monday" and "Tuesday." Continue on to the four columns on pages 6 and 7 with "Wednesday" through "Saturday," and take a day off on Sunday. On page 8 and

9 ("Triplets"), label the columns "Monday," "Tuesday," and "Wednesday," then on pages 10 through 12 ("Short Roll Combinations"), again label the columns "Monday" through "Saturday." Page 13 ("Review of Short Roll Combinations") is marked "Daily," and should conclude each daily practice session. So, a typical Monday session should include the first column on pages 5, 8, and 10, and all of page 13; a Thursday session would include the second column on pages 6 and 11 and all of page 13, and so forth. This is a great way to build technique, especially during the summer months or extended holidays when there is extra time off. It is especially helpful in building and maintaining your frame drumming chops. This is the all-important marinade. Your chops (and your audience) will thank you later!

Once a player's technique has been established, an abbreviated regimen can be applied using only the exercises that work both sides of the body. Please resist the temptation to go directly to these shortcuts! These are to be used only as maintenance exercises once a fairly complete technique has been attained. Simply circle the following selections in *Stick Control*:

Page 5: ex. 5–8, 13, 16–18, 23–24

Page 6: ex. 25–27, 32, 35–36, 39–40, 47–48

Page 7: ex. 53–54, 60–62, 69

Pages 8, 10, 11, 12: ex. 5–7, 12, 17–19, 24

Page 9: ex. 5–7

Standard rudimental snare drum solos such as "The General," "Hell on the Wabash," "Downfall of Paris," and "Connecticut Halftime," as well as selections from *N.A.R.D. Drum Solos* (Chicago: Ludwig Music Publishing, 1962) provide excellent material for developing frame drum technique and endurance. My students know their chops are beginning to cook when they can play "Three Camps" with all repeats on a frame drum. See how this recipe enhances your playing of the available solo material or traditional Arabic rhythms and improvisations.

Bon appétit!

Recipe for a Thinking Musician

She-e Wu

Music should never be just a mechanical activity. We need to have our minds focused on music all the time, whether we are playing or not.

INGREDIENTS:
Clear and focused brain
Open mind
Well-equipped hands
Sensitive and flexible ears
Big heart
Soul
Season to taste

SERVES:
All musicians.

Cooking time required
Lifetime

Step 1. Listen to as much music as you can. Listen with an analytical mind and your soul. The purpose behind listening to music varies, depending on whether one is a non-musician or a professional. Most human beings listen to music for pleasure—be it through live music or iPod recordings. Some people listen to music to learn, seeking something new or simply different from what they are used to. Some listen to music to be inspired. Others listen to music for escape. Listening to music provides the same effect as watching a movie: It takes you temporarily out of your everyday life to a different place. The unique aspect about listening to music is that the sound only exists in the airwave (not even in a solid form), and yet it has such a profound effect on us humans. It is the intangible nature of music that makes it a source of wonder and awe.

Step 2. Study subjects regarding music theory, music history, performance-practice. Most importantly, *use* what you learn *in* your music-making. The connection between what people know and what people use is often lost. Musicians sometimes go through music school focusing narrowly on a small repertory of pieces for their instrument. Only later do they realize that music school offered much more, and they regret the fact that they didn't take full advantage of studying a wide range of subjects when they had a chance. This includes yours truly!

Step 3. Use your imagination in the music. For example: Serene, Pesante, Animato, and Procelloso—each word should mean something different to you. Instead of ignoring composers' indications outright and going one's way, one should try to use the words to establish a link between the composer and the audience. It is similar to when we are reminded of someone or something when coming across a particular scent or spice. Try to connect your imagination to music making, because it is only through your imagination that you can bring those printed black notes on the white paper to life. The notation is a link to the creative act of music-making.

Step 4. Sing the music all the time. You can sing it in your head or sing it aloud. It is one of the best ways to explore and determine how to phrase. Now, I must admit that my own singing is not something I would want the public to hear. But I sing the music I play all the time, because it is the best way to sense its expressive power.

Step 5. Think about the music—the way you hear it and the way you want it to sound. Make the music happen while you play. Quite frequently, when I ask percussionists what they are thinking about when they play, many answer, "I don't know," or "nothing," or "hmm...." If one is not thinking about the very piece of music while one is playing it, then what is one thinking about? Dinner? A recent television show? Doing the laundry? When *should* one think about music that one is playing, if not during the performance? (See Step 9)

Step 6. Discuss music with other musicians, and not just percussionists. When you are filled with your own opinions and thoughts, you often find yourself wrapped up in your own world. As a result, you are not able to stay open-minded. A discussion with another musician can be inspiring, motivating, provoking, and possibly upsetting. That, however, is precisely what makes us grow.

Step 7. Listen to your own playing while you play. Watch and analyze *how* you are playing. Consider sound, tone, dynamics, tempo, phrasing, pacing, cadencing, expression markings, imagery, and the overall picture. Recording yourself helps, of course. But actively listening to yourself while you are playing is better, and active listening is critical for a refined performance. Only by listening to your playing actively, during the course of a performance, can you make changes immediately and appropriately.

Step 8. Observe and learn from other musicians. Who's your musical idol? How does she or he play? Scrutinize great musicians and see how they interpret, connect, or pace the music they play. Listen for the sound they produce from their instruments. Examine the technique they use. Watch how they move their body in relation to their music-making. Pay attention to their facial expression.

Whether it is something you want to model or something you don't care for, there is much to learn from others. It is said that when Bach assigned keyboard pieces to his students, he would first play through the work to give them a sense of how the music should sound and how it should be performed. Don't be afraid to model after the best.

Step 9. Think about the music you play *all the time*. Music-making is an intense and all-absorbing business. Think about the music *before* you can play it, *while* you are learning it, *when* you are not actively practicing it, *during* your performance, and also *after* your performance. Think about it even when you believe you know how you want it done. And just when you think you've thought enough, think some more. There is no end-point in music-thinking.

Caution: I do not recommend that you think about music intensely while driving or handling sharp objects, since that might cause accidents. However, at just about all other times, *think* about music. It's the best way to become a convincing musician. ➤

A Recipe for Success!

Zoro

Below is my personal recipe that I have used to attain and maintain success in absolutely every area of my life. All of the successes I have experienced in the past 25 years have required the same ingredients. The only difference has been the specifics of the goal itself, but the formula has always remained the same. If applied, I believe that you, too, can experience tremendous joy and a sense of fulfillment that comes from seeing your dreams come to fruition. Over the years I have shared this strategy with countless others who also have attained the success they dreamed of. If you can dream it, and are willing to work hard enough, you can have it. The key is to keep the dream alive in your heart and to work diligently and strategically toward the vision without ever entertaining the possibility of defeat.

Success, to me, is much more than fame, fortune, notoriety, or critical acclaim. True success for me is much deeper and encompasses all areas of life, both personal and professional. My deepest sense of satisfaction comes from doing what I know I was designed to do. The whole point of success is to find the purpose in what you do, rather than the task of what you do. To bring people joy through my instrument and encouragement through the art of communication is my purpose. I want to encourage you to find your purpose and live to fulfill that purpose. So here we go!

INGREDIENTS:
Vision
Purpose
Diligence
Perseverance
Patience
Attitude
Faith, Hope and Expectancy

SERVES:
This recipe will serve absolutely anyone who follows it!

Instructions
Stir all the above ingredients in equal amounts slowly in your heart, mind, soul, and body and let the mixture simmer over the course of your lifetime. Then patiently await, and an amazing and delightfully satisfying aroma will eventually engulf you. The smell will be that of sweet success. Like a fine wine, some things taste better given more time. Success is one of those things. The longer it takes to achieve something, the more we appreciate it when we finally get there. It's like the difference between fast-food meals as compared to a carefully crafted culinary creation. Real success takes time and lots of it. It takes years to develop the

necessary skills needed for success. And it takes wisdom to discern how best to employ those skills. A very complex process, really.

Vision

Without exception, each of my dreams exploded in my heart first and eventually made it to my head. You must get the vision from your heart to your head and then get it on paper. I still have drafts of some of my original visions and dreams from 25 years ago. All have come to pass. Some took a few years, others a decade, still others 20 to 25 years, and even more are coming to pass as I write this. The way I figure it, time is going to pass anyway, so it may as well pass as I am steadily and faithfully moving uphill toward the goal.

Once you have a vision, you need a compass by which to navigate. For example, there are many ways one can travel from Los Angeles to New York City, many modes of transportation, and many roads if you travel by car. If you are wise, you will use a map to help you decide how you want to get there. Long-range and short-range goals help you to navigate the best use of your time and resources based on your vision. It doesn't mean that you always get there in a straight line, but you have a much better chance of getting there by careful planning than by just winging it and getting tossed in whatever direction the wind blows. That's a real hard way to navigate a ship that has a destination.

Don't forget to make decrees or declarations over your life because words have power. We are shaped for better or worse by the words we speak. I have always spoken of success as if it were something that was inevitable. And I would talk about it as a matter of when, not if. I have always made decrees over my life. In other words, make positive confessions of what you want to see come about. Positive images conceived in your heart, released through your mouth, and walked out, eventually find a place in your reality. The power of positive thinking cannot be underrated, because images in your mind have substance in an unseen realm. They possess the invisible power to lead you to the desired destination.

Purpose

For me, having a purpose has always been vital. As an educator, clinician, and speaker my sole purpose is to educate, inspire, and motivate, because that is what I am wired for. The purpose of my drumming was to serve the artists that I played for. The sum total of what you do should be much more than an activity of self-absorption. When I am flowing in my gifting, others are built up because my purpose is to build up others. My particular gifts, whether it's playing, speaking, or writing, are the means by which I accomplish it.

Diligence

Every one has talent and gifting, but only the wise exercise the necessary discipline to develop them. You are the gatekeeper of your own success, the steward over your own desires. Diligence is a choice. It is not something that comes automatically. You must choose to labor hard to develop your craft and take it to the highest level possible. This is just good old-fashioned work—blood, sweat and tears.

Perseverance

I would be lying if I told you that I did not experience discouragement countless times while in pursuit of my dreams. Trials, tribulations, setbacks, and disappointments have all been part of my journey. In fact, they are to be expected. But I have never looked at failure as a permanent destination, only a temporary address on the way to success. You must make a decision in advance to endure until you see the manifestation of what you have dreamed. I am living proof that it can be done.

Successful people are no more talented than unsuccessful people, they are just people who refused to give up. I have been unwilling to give up and absolutely relentless in terms of moving forward in the storms of my life. All of my growth has come in times of testing. We all love the times of prosperity and peace, but true growth only comes in times of testing and adversity. Only under the pressure of battles is a warrior refined. If you endure and are open, you will learn more than ever in these times and eventually look back with satisfaction and gratitude for these important and necessary times. Adversity builds character and character builds success. Gifting can get you to the top, but character will keep you there.

Patience

Patience is a huge part of diligence and the least embraced and understood. Nothing great on the earth was built quickly. Just observe all things in creation and you will see how every great thing starts of as a small seed, and over time, becomes huge, like a giant sequoia tree, for instance. We are no different. In fact, the maturation period for a human being is the slowest of all living creatures. Many dreams are unrealized due to a lack of patience. Most people quit just shy of their breakthrough. Patience can be developed. None of us like it, but it is absolutely essential if you ever want to achieve anything worthwhile.

Attitude

Your attitude is the single most important determining factor of your success. The key is to maintain a positive attitude throughout the good times and the bad times. If I could sum up in one word the key to my own success it would be *humility*. Humility allows me to be corrected; it is the portal to wisdom from those who know more than I. And make no mistake, wisdom does not come automatically with age, wisdom is a choice and humility is how you access wisdom. You must choose humility and keep it in your heart. It's how you will improve and perfect your skills in the most rapid manner.

Faith, Hope and Expectancy

All of my successes have come from my ability to live in denial! By that I mean that when you're in the pursuit of a dream, the obstacles, barriers, and challenges always seem impossible to overcome. I have learned to live in denial by learning to see the future through the eyes of faith and to look past the present circumstances. In other words, believing in advance that something is possible, even if at the present moment it seems impossible.

Most people live by the phrase "seeing is believing." I have lived by the opposite motto: "believing is seeing!" In other words, I learned to see it in my mind's eye and refused to change the channel. It's not to say that doubts and fears didn't steadily surface. It's just that I pushed on in spite of them. I learned to be motivated by faith, not fear.

From geographical expeditions, to great military victories, to amazing innovations, anyone who has achieved greatness in any area of human history would tell you that with faith all things are possible, but with fear nothing is possible. I always believed that if I were persistent and patient, doors of opportunity would eventually open and skills would be developed.

I can honestly say that where I endured and did what was required, success and progress was inevitable. I was always hopeful and expecting that around every corner could be some tremendous breakthrough. That is called hope and expectancy and was not founded in a fairy tale mentality but founded in a practical strategic plan that was being diligently worked on day after day, month after month, and year after year.

In Conclusion

As the old adage goes, "the proof is in the pudding." These life principles have worked for me as a player, educator, author, producer, inventor, speaker, husband, father, and friend. It is my hope that they will inspire you to develop the limitless potential that lies within you so that you may experience a life worth living. I continue to apply these strategies to newer endeavors of my life with the same vigor, enthusiasm, and expectation as I have with all of my past accomplishments. I always look ahead to the future, and I remain open to change, which most people resist. Change is good and the only thing that will assure continued growth and challenge us as human beings.

Remember that success is not a destination, but rather a journey, so be sure to enjoy the journey and the process with all of its ups and downs. Don't be in a hurry to get to the finish line because there is none. Give life your all and give each day absolutely everything you have! Live passionately and on fire for the things that make you feel most alive.